RAND NATIONAL DEFENSE RESEARCH INSTITUTE

Improving DoD Support to FEMA's All-Hazards Plans

Michael J. McNerney, Christopher M. Schnaubelt,
Agnes Gereben Schaefer, Martina Melliand, Bill Gelfeld

Prepared for the Office of the Secretary of Defense

For more information on this publication, visit www.rand.org/t/rr1301

Library of Congress Control Number: 2015957729
ISBN: 978-0-8330-9219-9

Published by the RAND Corporation, Santa Monica, Calif.

Cover images courtesy of Staff Sgt. Jim Greenhill, National Guard Bureau; Walt Jennings/FEMA.

Preface

Disaster preparedness and response is a national priority, in which the U.S. Department of Defense (DoD) plays a supporting—but potentially crucial—role. In the ten years since Hurricane Katrina, the Federal Emergency Management Agency (FEMA) has taken steps to strengthen its ability to plan and coordinate the U.S. government's response to disasters, while DoD has worked to improve its support to FEMA.

This research reviews and analyzes how DoD and FEMA work together to plan and execute disaster response activities, and recommends areas for improvement.

This research was sponsored by the Office of the Assistant Secretary of Defense for Homeland Defense and Global Security. It was conducted within the International Security and Defense Policy Center of the RAND National Defense Research Institute, a federally funded research and development center sponsored by the Office of the Secretary of Defense, the Joint Staff, the Unified Combatant Commands, the Navy, the Marine Corps, the defense agencies, and the defense Intelligence Community.

For more information on the RAND International Security and Defense Policy Center, see http://www.rand.org/nsrd/ndri/centers/isdp.html or contact the director (contact information is provided on the web page).

Contents

Figures and Tables

Figures

Tables

Summary

U.S. national disaster response plans indicate that the U.S. Department of Defense (DoD) is generally considered to be a resource of last resort, to be called on when state resources are overwhelmed and alternative federal response assets are insufficient. Unless designated by the president, DoD is never the lead federal agency for civil support missions; it always operates in support of civil authorities, although it will maintain command and control over Title 10 military forces when deployed in support of a lead federal agency. Therefore, one of the biggest challenges for DoD is determining the capability requirements to best meet the needs of other federal agencies, which in turn are often reflections of needs identified by state, local, tribal, or territorial governments. This is especially true when responding to complex, large-scale incidents that require employment of military forces and other DoD capabilities.[1]

It can also be challenging for the Federal Emergency Management Agency (FEMA) to determine its own requirements across its ten geographic regions, which consist of sovereign states, especially when taking into account the varied capabilities outside the federal government. To the extent that FEMA can communicate federal response requirements and civilian response capabilities (including its own), common capability gaps can be identified, and planning can be conducted to address these gaps.

DoD can bring critical capabilities to a disaster response both in terms of specialization ("specificity") and mass ("quantity"), and DoD has significant capacity that can rapidly deploy with little external support. However, it must understand potential requirements as clearly as possible and build this understanding into its planning activities.

Approach

The objective of this research was to identify ways that DoD can better support FEMA. To achieve this objective, the study team (1) analyzed FEMA plans and DoD policies for Defense Support of Civil Authorities (DSCA); (2) analyzed how DoD provides DSCA support to FEMA, including key stakeholder perceptions, in order to identify potential capability gaps that DoD could fill; and (3) developed recommendations for how DoD can improve

[1] These may be complex catastrophes, defined by DoD as

> Any natural or man-made incident, including cyberspace attack, power grid failure, and terrorism, which results in cascading failures of multiple, interdependent, critical, life-sustaining infrastructure sectors and causes extraordinary levels of mass casualties, damage, or disruption severely affecting the population, environment, economy, public health, national morale, response efforts, and/or government functions. (Deputy Secretary of Defense, "Definition of the Term Complex Catastrophe," memorandum for Secretaries of the Military Departments, Washington, D.C., February 19, 2013)

Disasters of lesser scope may also require a substantial DoD response.

its support—in terms of planning, coordination, and providing requested capabilities—to FEMA.

We began by conducting a broad literature review that included analyzing DoD guidance and policy on DSCA, in addition to studying the National Response Framework, National Incident Management System, the 2011 National Preparedness Goal, and the 2013 National Preparedness Report, as well as other relevant Department of Homeland Security (DHS) and FEMA reports. We also conducted semistructured interviews with personnel from the Office of the Secretary of Defense (OSD), the Joint Staff, combatant commands (CCMDs), defense coordinating officers (DCOs) and defense coordinating elements (DCEs), and FEMA and performed an in-depth analysis of FEMA's ten regional all-hazards plans (AHPs) from the perspective of DoD support.

Per the scope of this work as defined by the sponsor, we considered only the employment of Title 10 federal military forces. Other than a brief consideration of dual-status command, we assumed that National Guard forces performing DSCA while on state active duty or operating under Title 32 would be state resources.[2]

Review of FEMA All-Hazards Plans and Identification of Potential Capability Gaps

Each of FEMA's ten regions is responsible for writing AHPs that guide response efforts in the wake of disasters, including large-scale catastrophes. The AHPs represent a critical tool in coordinating efforts to respond to large-scale catastrophes throughout the United States and its territories. They are a standardized way for FEMA to plan for response operations in each of its ten regions.

To better appreciate how DoD might fit into these plans and the scenarios covered, we analyzed all the available AHPs to determine the specific threats addressed and the capabilities and resources earmarked for response efforts. Additionally, we looked at the roles and resources requested of DoD by each region to identify opportunities to better coordinate the two organizations' concerted response to catastrophic incidents.[3] Our purpose was not to compare the plans or evaluate their quality per se but rather to assess whether they had sufficient information to identify capability gaps that DoD might fill. Table S.1 provides a snapshot of our analysis of the AHPs in their current iterations, as available on FEMA's WebEOC portal. A more detailed discussion of our analytic approach and our findings is in Chapter Two.

Assessment of FEMA Plans

There is considerable overlap in the types of support capabilities requested of DoD by the ten FEMA regions. These requests relate to particular emergency support functions (ESFs) and

---

[2] See Joint Publication 3-28, *Defense Support of Civil Authorities*, Washington, D.C.: Joint Chiefs of Staff, July 2013, pp. I-6, II-2 through II-5, and Appendix D; and Army Doctrine Reference Publication 3-28, *Defense Support of Civil Authorities*, Washington, D.C.: Department of the Army, June 2013, pp. II-8 and II-9, for discussion of various authorities for use of National Guard forces for DSCA.

[3] The National Response Framework defines a catastrophic incident as "any natural or manmade incident, including terrorism, that results in extraordinary levels of mass casualties, damage, or disruption severely affecting the population, infrastructure, environment, economy, national morale, or government functions" (DHS, *National Response Framework*, 2nd edition, Washington, D.C., May 2013, p. 1).

Table S.1
DoD Requirements in FEMA All-Hazards Plans

Region	Threat Analysis Included	Role of DoD Adequately Explained to Enable Planning	Specific DoD Resources/ Quantities Requested	Large-Scale Catastrophes Addressed	Overall Impression
I	Yes	Yes	Yes/Yes	Major threats and necessary responses thoroughly detailed	• Comprehensive list of plans and contingencies in each state • Contains an extensive tasking of DoD resources—specifically tasks roles and resources • Targeted response capabilities and expectations for disasters • Tailored to major catastrophes
II	Yes	Yes	Some	Somewhat—tsunami ISP for Puerto Rico/U.S. Virgin Islands in progress	• Reasonably thorough • Missing specific scenario plans
III	No	No	No/No	No	• Contains only sketches of responsibilities and divisions of task • No specific guidance for DoD
IV	Yes	Yes	Yes/No	No ISPs, but hurricanes and other threats directly addressed	• Comprehensive detailed plan of how to implement emergency protocol in every situation • State-by-state breakdown provides detailed information
V	Yes	Somewhat	Yes/No	No ISPs, but detailed fact sheet on major types of threats	• Detailed lists of phases and tasks (with similar checklists) • Limited concrete support tasks for DoD and little specificity for actions • Conducted major improvised nuclear device exercise in 2013
VI	Yes	Yes	Yes/Yes	No ISPs, but major threats directly addressed	• Detailed plan with specific threats and types/quantities of DoD resources specified • Clear expectations of DoD
VII	No	No	No/No	Detailed, specific New Madrid Seismic Zone Plan in place for Missouri but region-wide ISP still not available	• Plan barely addresses role of DoD • Few if any resources mentioned • Reviews ESFs but provides only broad information
VIII	Not Finalized/Not Available				

Table S.1—Continued

Region	Threat Analysis Included	Role of DoD Adequately Explained to Enable Planning	Specific DoD Resources/ Quantities Requested	Large-Scale Catastrophes Addressed	Overall Impression
IX	Somewhat	No	No/No	Detailed, thorough ISPs for Southern California and Northern California earthquakes and tsunamis and Hawaii and Guam catastrophe plans	• Role of DoD (DCO/DCE) only vaguely mentioned in support capacity for broad missions • Lacks specificity
X	Somewhat	No	No/No	Somewhat—ISP in progress for Cascadia Subduction Zone earthquake	• Provides only a cursory sketch of roles and responsibilities with little information on task breakdowns, resources, or role of DoD

Key:

Thorough and complete; comprehensive plan.

Reasonably thorough and complete; some missing sections or information.

Not thorough or complete; missing a lot of information; lacks specificity.

often represent more complex logistical capabilities that the regions do not consider themselves capable of handling without external support. The requested DoD capabilities most often fall under the following general categories:

- Transportation (ESF #1)
- Communications (ESF #2)
- Airlift and evacuation support (ESF #5)
- Search and rescue (SAR) (ESF #5)
- Logistics (ESF #7)
- Base installation support (ESF #7)
- Mass care/medical support (ESF #8)
- Mass fatality management (ESF #8).

In addition to the AHPs, several regions have also written incident-specific plans (ISPs), which highlight particular dangers and scenarios endemic to the region. These ISPs provide detailed responses for large-scale catastrophes, including earthquakes in Region VII (New Madrid Seismic Zone), Region IX (in Northern and Southern California), and Region X (Cascadia Subduction Zone—plan in progress), as well as tsunamis in Region II (Puerto Rico and the U.S. Virgin Islands—plan in progress) and Region IX (Hawaii and Guam). These plans offer specific, tailored guidance for the most likely high-level threats each region faces.

Recommendations to Improve FEMA Plans

From our review of these plans, as well as our wider review of the disaster preparedness literature and our interviews with subject-matter experts, we identified the following recommendations.

Clear expectations for types and numbers of resources are critical for DoD to be able to fully support FEMA in the wake of a disaster, particularly a large-scale catastrophe. DoD should consider initiating a series of small, focused workshops with FEMA officials to discuss remaining information gaps and ways to close them, as well as ways to make expectations on both sides more explicit and understood. While requests are submitted from FEMA to DoD in the form of capabilities, it would help DoD planners to know what specific resources might be needed or expected, while still affording DoD flexibility and discretion in response. The AHPs might be more useful to DoD planning if scenarios referenced the need for specific capabilities in the form of approximate numbers (e.g., weights, distances, personnel) that might be requested by the FEMA regions, with the understanding that these would be rough estimates for planning purposes.

Additionally, DoD (as well as other agencies engaged in disaster response) would benefit from a listing of specific actions and capabilities in the face of large-scale catastrophes. In most regions, FEMA has solid procedures and checklists in place. However, apart from the "entirety of DoD" through the Global Force Management (GFM) process, it is not as clear where the additional resources and assets (both material and personnel) to implement these plans will come from in the event of a catastrophe. The ISPs that do exist are fairly detailed in identifying requirements for DoD and could be used as exemplars. Several other region-specific ISPs are still in progress or unavailable. These plans will provide key guidance in the event of a catastrophe, so DoD might wish to identify opportunities to facilitate their development.[4]

Review of DSCA Support Provided by DoD to FEMA

To help assess how DoD support to FEMA regional planning might be improved, we interviewed more than two dozen military officers and civilian officials assigned to OSD, the Joint Staff, U.S. Northern Command (USNORTHCOM), U.S. Pacific Command (USPACOM), National Guard Bureau (NGB), U.S. Army North (ARNORTH), and Army G3/Western Hemisphere Emergency Management (WHEM; formerly Directorate of Military Support—DOMS). We also spoke with two different DCOs and members of three DCEs, and observed DCE-FEMA region staff interactions during the FEMA Region II Trade Winds Hurricane Exercise during the first week of June 2015.

Best Practices in DSCA Support to FEMA

The following are areas in which our assessment—shared by many stakeholders we interviewed—is that DoD support to FEMA regional planning is working well, and DoD should consider sustaining and even building on them. This is not an all-inclusive list but highlights areas that were particularly notable during interviews and research into current plans and recent exercise experiences.

---

[4] In concert with CCMD planners and DCOs/DCEs, FEMA has established sets of pre-scripted mission assignments (PSMAs). As discussed below, perceptions regarding the utility of PSMAs varied widely among the stakeholders we interviewed.

DoD Integration with FEMA Planning

Interviewees from both CCMDs stated that interagency coordination and planning was a significant aspect of their missions. They have exchanged liaison officers with FEMA headquarters and have staff directorates that are specifically dedicated to interagency coordination. USNORTHCOM and USPACOM are integrated with FEMA regional planning through both the DCO for each region and through additional support from the CCMD planning staffs. Both have robust concept of operations plans (CONPLANs) for DSCA, with several scenarios/playbooks already completed and, in the case of USNORTHCOM, many others in development. USNORTHCOM and USPACOM have identified gaps in some FEMA regional plans and have established milestones to develop additional plans to provide DoD capabilities where needed. DCOs and DCE personnel with planning responsibility receive several weeks of training on DSCA planning, including courses conducted by ARNORTH and by FEMA.[5]

Logistics Support Planning

USNORTHCOM's Mobility Division staff works closely with FEMA to get advance notice if it appears likely that strategic airlift will be needed. The Interagency Transportation Support Framework concept of operations was developed to ensure FEMA crisis response teams are properly trained on preparing their cargo for movement on DoD aircraft. FEMA personnel are trained on a space-available basis at DoD installations on pallet buildup, hazardous material documentation, and cargo load plans. The USNORTHCOM/USPACOM Joint Logistics Operations Center supports the FEMA national logistics coordinator. They are developing an installation usage guide that addresses logistics functional capabilities and helps to choose base support installations and identify conflicts in demand between base support installations and federal staging areas.[6] Bringing stakeholders together, such as the National Guard, federal reserve components, and FEMA, they discovered many that stakeholders had planned to use the same bases and would have exceeded their capacity. USNORTHCOM logistics planners stated that their approach is to give FEMA requirements priority and then deconflict the plans of the National Guard and federal military forces for use of federal bases while documenting state National Guard plans for life support areas.[7] The USPACOM approach is slightly different in that it has to analyze the impact of its support to FEMA on its military readiness and strategic plans.

DoD Participation in FEMA Exercises

USNORTHCOM, USPACOM, and their DCOs routinely participate in FEMA exercises at the regional level, and the DCOs often participate in state-level exercises. Lessons from such participation are developed through the after action review process and subsequently used by CCMD staff to refine DSCA plans.

Key Challenges in DSCA Support to FEMA

These are areas in which we assess that DoD support to FEMA regional planning could be improved, which has implications for changes in processes, policies, and/or authorities.

---

5 For a list of courses, see U.S. Army North, Defense Support of Civil Authorities (DSCA) website, undated.

6 Base support installations are locations designated for DoD forces to perform reception, staging, onward movement, and integration. Federal staging areas are locations where civilian responders plan to conduct staging activities.

7 Interview with USNORTHCOM personnel, December 16, 2014.

Conflicting Perceptions Within DoD of the Relative Priority of DSCA[8]

Interviews with DoD stakeholders indicated that different organizations had different perceptions regarding the priority of DSCA versus warfighting. Several interviewees assigned to the Joint Staff emphasized that DSCA is a lesser-priority mission.[9] Regarding support to FEMA regional planning, they stated that, in most cases, DoD has already identified its capabilities for catastrophic incidents.[10] For the scenarios that are exceptions, interviewees stated that DoD should wait for FEMA to complete its own ongoing planning before providing planning assistance. They posited that a massive catastrophe, such as inundation from a tsunami caused by an earthquake in the Cascadia Subduction Zone, would be disastrous, but because it has a very low probability in the next three to five years, "we can afford to have strategic patience."[11] Some stakeholders noted that the Joint Staff itself has reduced its emphasis on DSCA in recent years.[12]

Interviewees at OSD and USNORTHCOM, however, disputed the idea that DSCA is a secondary mission. While acknowledging that DoD capabilities for DSCA should be dual-use and acquired for warfighting requirements, they argued that DoD's *Strategy for Homeland Defense and Defense Support of Civil Authorities* and a 2012 Secretary of Defense memorandum titled "Actions to Improve Defense Support in Complex Catastrophes" provide clear guidance that DSCA is a priority.[13]

While the 2015 *National Military Strategy* ranks DSCA as number 11 in a list of 12, DSCA nonetheless makes the list of joint force prioritized missions.[14]

Sourcing of DoD Forces for DSCA Missions

Several USNORTHCOM interviewees advocated for more assigned forces to support the DSCA mission. Otherwise, they argued, too much time is consumed by the GFM process. USNORTHCOM interviewees suggested that a system of "geographically proximate sourcing" should be developed to speed up employment time.

OSD and Joint Staff interviewees disagreed with these assertions, but from different perspectives. Some Joint Staff personnel said that the normal GFM process would be speeded up in case of a catastrophe but that FEMA should be informed not to expect federal military forces in less than 72 to 96 hours in the case of a no-notice event.[15] OSD staff stated that, in the event of a no-notice catastrophe, sourcing could be accelerated through the use of a Secretary

---

[8] We describe the disparities we found between the viewpoints of various parts of DoD because the sponsor expressed interest in this topic. However, adjudicating them is beyond the scope of this effort.

[9] Interviews with Joint Staff personnel, October 24, 2014, November 7, 2014, and November 19, 2014. In a subsequent communication, Joint Staff personnel provided the following explication: "DSCA is provided by DoD, at time of incident, when requested, and within capabilities. DSCA may become higher priority at time of incident, depending upon the nature of event and competing global demands."

[10] USNORTHCOM and USPACOM DSCA plans are discussed in detail within the body of this report.

[11] Interview with Joint Staff personnel, November 19, 2014.

[12] Multiple interviews in 2014 and 2015.

[13] DoD, *Strategy for Homeland Defense and Defense Support of Civil Authorities*, Washington, D.C., February 2013; Secretary of Defense, "Actions to Improve Defense Support in Complex Catastrophes," memorandum, July 20, 2012.

[14] Joint Chiefs of Staff, *The National Military Strategy of the United States of America*, Washington, D.C., 2015.

[15] Interview with Joint Staff personnel, October 24, 2014.

of Defense special orders book and that geographic proximity is already accepted as a selection criterion for DSCA sourcing through a program called Preferred Force Generation.[16]

Conflicting Objectives of DSCA Exercises Between DoD and FEMA

Virtually all interviewees stated that interagency exercises were productive and regularly used to test DSCA plans. CCMD staffs frequently use after action reviews to identify the need for adjustments to DSCA plans. However, some FEMA officials perceived a divergence between DoD and FEMA objectives for emergency response exercises.

Interviews with DCE personnel appeared to validate this perception.[17] They reported that FEMA and DoD personnel have different cultures in regard to planning, and this is naturally reflected in how plans are exercised.[18] DoD personnel tend to be interested in scenarios that include unexpected events and test contingency plans, while FEMA personnel wish to focus on executing a planned scenario and rehearsing established processes. Nonetheless, while recognizing these differences in approach, DoD interviewees at multiple levels stated they had not experienced any significant problems in meeting both FEMA and military organizational objectives during exercises.[19]

Dual-Status Commander Construct

Nonfederalized National Guard forces, i.e., those operating in a state active duty or U.S. Title 32 status, provide support to state emergency management agencies under the command of their respective governors. Because the National Guard consists of military forces, even though they are not normally on federal active duty, a chain of command that reports to a state governor instead of the president of the United States presents a challenge to unity of effort. The construct of a dual-status commander (DSC) to link federal and state chains of command was developed as a command-and-control option to address this dilemma. Most interviewees posited that the appointment of a DSC has apparently worked thus far, but several asserted that the construct has not been adequately tested in multistate catastrophes.

Lack of Visibility into Installation- and Unit-Level Immediate Response Plans

Although commanders implementing immediate response must report their activity through their unit chain of command, virtually all the key DSCA stakeholders we interviewed indicated that their organizations had no visibility on installation and unit plans for carrying out immediate response as authorized by DoD Directive (DoDD) 3025.18, *Defense Support of Civil Authorities*.[20]

---

[16] Interviews with OSD personnel, November 24, 2014, February 5, 2015, and May 19, 2015; interview with G3/Western Hemisphere Emergency Management personnel, April 16, 2015. Preferred Force Generation and an add-on capability called Joint Capability Support to National Emergencies are discussed in greater detail later in this report.

[17] Interviews with DCE personnel, June 3, 2015.

[18] It is unclear whether state emergency response organizations have a planning culture that is more similar to FEMA or DoD's culture or that is distinct from both. Although it was outside the scope of this effort, to the extent that unmet state needs may drive FEMA resource requirements, it may be equally useful to understand this culture.

[19] Interviews with USNORTHCOM personnel, December 16, 2014; interviews with G3/WHEM personnel, April 16, 2015; interviews with DCE personnel, June 3, 2015.

[20] DoDD 3025.18, *Defense Support of Civil Authorities (DSCA)*, Washington, D.C., September 21, 2012.

Recommendations for Improving DoD Support to FEMA

We recommend consideration of the following specific actions:

For OSD/Joint Staff/services:

- Publish an update of DoDD 3025.18 that consolidates guidance issued since September 2012, including the relative priority of DSCA within the 2015 *National Military Strategy*, and states that complex catastrophes are DoD's main effort for DSCA planning.
- Issue guidance requiring commanders implementing Immediate Response Authority to maximize communication, including by informing the appropriate DCO at the same time as their service chain of command.
- Issue guidance requiring services to consolidate information from installation emergency management programs of domestic installations under their authority and provide this information to the appropriate CCMD on an annual basis.
- Consider advocating for an increase in the relative priority of the DSCA mission as it relates to complex catastrophes to place it on par with military defense of the homeland.
- Institutionalize DSCA liaison personnel integration with FEMA planning within the forthcoming DoD instruction that will address liaisons (DoDI 3025.jj).
- Reassess DCO/DCE staffing to consider directing the services to increase the personnel authorizations for regions with greater risks, as well as making them joint organizations.
- Consider apportioning additional forces for USNORTHCOM plans for complex catastrophes, or otherwise implement a mechanism to authorize direct liaison between USNORTHCOM and major commands likely to provide forces in such cases.
- Consider accelerating development of the Joint Staff's Joint Capability Support to National Emergencies (JCStoNE) system to improve DoD's ability to provide forces, and engage with FEMA in its development.
- Test the principle of unity of effort (including roles of Title 10 forces, DSCs, etc.) in a multistate complex catastrophe through smaller-scale or tabletop exercises. Incorporate legal considerations into exercise designs to evaluate the potential need for additional legal authority.
- Work with FEMA to help develop and document its approach to identifying shortfalls and requirements more accurately to ensure rapid, effective DSCA.

For USNORTHCOM/USPACOM:

- Sustain logistics support planning coordination with FEMA, particularly to deconflict federal military, National Guard, and FEMA use of resources such as base support installations/federal staging areas.
- Do more to socialize logistic support planning efforts with FEMA and other parts of the civilian response community.
- DoD and FEMA officials should coordinate on exercise design earlier to ensure both agencies' objectives are accomplished.
- Continue to provide CCMD staff planning assistance to FEMA regions—including for AHPs—to complement/augment DCO/DCE planning support.
- USNORTHCOM should complete the regional support plans under CONPLAN 3500-14 and routinize its review in the Chairman's Readiness System.

Acknowledgments

The authors would like to especially thank Robert G. Salesses, the Deputy Assistant Secretary of Defense for Homeland Defense Integration and Defense Support of Civil Authorities, who sponsored this project, and Joseph J. McMenamin, who, as Principal Director, Homeland Defense Integration and Defense Support of Civil Authorities, provided much of the initial guidance for its research design. We are also grateful for the support of Mr. Salesses's special assistant, Matthew M. Gula, who provided important feedback throughout the effort and was invaluable in helping to coordinate interviews and obtain copies of official documents.

COL Wes McClellan and COL Ed Larkin in NGB J3/7 were very helpful in providing information on National Guard DSCA planning and procedures. Kenneth Rome, the Vice Deputy Director for Regional Operations and Force Management in Joint Staff J3, helped us obtain the most current information regarding procedures for sourcing DSCA forces. Maj Gen John F. Newell III, Director of Strategy, Policy and Plans (J5), and Randel Zeller, Director of Interagency Coordination (J9) at USNORTHCOM/North American Aerospace Defense Command (NORAD), provided important support, providing information on USNORTHCOM DSCA planning. Darah M. Hyland, Chief of the Interagency Strategy & Plans Branch NORAD and USNORTHCOM/J955, helped coordinate our interviews at USNORTHCOM and provided insights on FEMA regional plans. Mario Costagliola, the Operations Planner for Defense Coordinating Element, U.S. Army North Region II, assisted in coordinating DCO/DCE interviews and making arrangements to observe the FEMA Trade Winds exercise. COL Debra Rice and her staff at Army G34/WHEM were extremely helpful, providing data on DSCA planning and sourcing, as well as the request-for-assistance decision process. We also thank our interviewees from FEMA for their valuable insights on FEMA's planning process and interagency coordination mechanisms.

We greatly appreciate the support of our RAND colleagues: Seth Jones and Henry Willis for their leadership; Bear McConnell and Major Jerry VanVactor for their sage advice; Betsy Kammer for her administrative support; and James Torr and Beth Bernstein for their editorial expertise. We would like to also thank our reviewers, VADM Robert Parker, U.S. Coast Guard (Retired), and Gary Cecchine, for their valuable feedback. Finally, we would like to thank the many DoD and FEMA personnel who shared their knowledge and insights in nonattribution interviews. We could not have completed this work without their candid participation.

CHAPTER ONE

Introduction

Background and Purpose

While the federal government's role in disaster response goes back to the 19th century, disaster planning by the federal government began in 1979 with the establishment of the Federal Emergency Management Agency (FEMA). The 1988 Stafford Disaster Relief and Emergency Assistance Act (Pub. L. 93-288) established the system within which federal agencies—including the U.S. Department of Defense (DoD)—assist state and local governments. The Stafford Act put FEMA in charge of developing a federal response plan and required states to develop emergency response plans. Response planning continued to improve in subsequent years with adoption of an all-hazards approach and, in 2004, the development of the National Response Plan.[1]

The challenges confronted in responding to Hurricane Katrina in August 2005, however, served as a wake-up call as to how far planners still had to go. The Post-Katrina Emergency Management Reform Act of 2006 (Pub. L. 109-295) dramatically changed how the government carries out this crucial responsibility.[2] In addition to many other changes, the act helped drive a more comprehensive, synchronized approach to planning, best illustrated by the 2008 National Response Framework (NRF).[3] The NRF helped clarify disaster planning and response roles across all levels of government, as well as for stakeholders outside government, and it required completion of both strategic and operational plans for specific incident scenarios.

DoD has a long history of assisting domestic civil authorities in responding to disasters. In some cases, DoD has been called on to provide capabilities that do not exist or are unavailable elsewhere. DoD historically has been called on to provide additional common capabilities (e.g., troops, vehicles, doctors) and unique ones (e.g., chemical, biological, radiological, nuclear [CBRN]). In recent years, it has also provided increasing support through its expertise in strategic and operational planning.

However, it is widely recognized that the response to most natural disasters begins at the local level, and that is how response assets are arranged. National response planning documents have directed an escalating response, from local or regional to state and, finally, federal response. Therefore, federal capabilities are generally provided in response to a disaster only

[1] U.S. Department of Homeland Security (DHS), *National Response Plan*, Washington, D.C., December 2004.

[2] Public Law 109-295, Post-Katrina Emergency Management Reform Act, October 4, 2006.

[3] DHS, *National Response Framework*, 1st edition, Washington, D.C., January 2008.

when requested by a state governor or when the President of the United States has declared a major disaster.[4]

Under the current NRF, like the response planning documents that preceded it, DoD is generally considered to be a resource of last resort that is to be called on only when state resources are overwhelmed and alternative federal response assets are insufficient. Unless designated by the President, DoD is never the lead federal agency for Defense Support of Civil Authorities (DSCA) missions; it always operates in support of civil authorities, although it will maintain command and control over Title 10 military forces when deployed in support of a lead federal agency. Therefore, one of the biggest challenges for DoD is determining the capability requirements to best meet the needs of other federal agencies, which in turn may be driven by needs identified by state and local governments. This is especially true when responding to complex, large-scale incidents that require employment of military forces and other DoD capabilities in a federal response.[5] It can also be difficult for FEMA to determine its own requirements across its ten geographic regions, especially when taking into account the varied capabilities outside the federal government. To the extent FEMA can clearly and explicitly communicate federal response requirements and civilian response capabilities (including its own), common capability gaps can be identified. DoD can bring critical capabilities to a response, both in terms of specialization ("specificity") and mass ("quantity"). Thus, it is important for DoD to understand potential requirements as clearly as possible and build this understanding into its support planning. In the ten years since Hurricane Katrina, FEMA has taken many steps to improve disaster preparedness, particularly in such areas as planning and U.S. government coordination. The introduction of all-hazards plans (AHPs) by FEMA regions marked an opportunity for DoD planners to add greater specificity to their own support plans and to strengthen coordination with FEMA. In light of these developments, the Office of the Assistant Secretary of Defense for Homeland Defense and Global Security asked RAND to analyze DoD efforts to support FEMA and to identify opportunities for improvements.

Approach

The objective of this research was to identify ways that DoD can better support FEMA. To achieve that objective, we (1) analyzed FEMA plans and DoD policies for DSCA; (2) analyzed how DoD provides support to FEMA, including by documenting key stakeholder perceptions, in order to identify potential capability gaps that DoD could fill; and (3) developed recommendations for how DoD can improve its support to FEMA.

We began by conducting a broad literature review that included analyzing DoD guidance and policy on DSCA, in addition to studying the NRF, National Incident Management

---

[4] Public Law 93-288, Robert T. Stafford Disaster Relief and Emergency Assistance Act, November 23, 1988.

[5] These may be complex catastrophes, defined by DoD as

> Any natural or man-made incident, including cyberspace attack, power grid failure, and terrorism, which results in cascading failures of multiple, interdependent, critical, life-sustaining infrastructure sectors and causes extraordinary levels of mass casualties, damage, or disruption severely affecting the population, environment, economy, public health, national morale, response efforts, and/or government functions. (Deputy Secretary of Defense, "Definition of the Term Complex Catastrophe," memorandum for Secretaries of the Military Departments, Washington, D.C., February 19, 2013)

Disasters of lesser scope may also require a substantial DoD response.

System, the 2011 National Preparedness Goal, and the 2013 National Preparedness Report, as well as other relevant DHS and FEMA reports.

We also conducted semistructured interviews with personnel from the Office of the Secretary of Defense (OSD), the Joint Staff, combatant commands (CCMDs), defense coordinating officers (DCOs) and defense coordinating elements (DCEs), and FEMA. These interviews allowed us to analyze current planning and coordination mechanisms between DoD and FEMA and identify ways in which those might be improved. Individuals we interviewed were assigned to offices and organizations that included the following:

- FEMA
  - Response Directorate
  - Office of Response and Recovery
  - National Continuity Programs
- OSD
  - Deputy Assistant Secretary of Defense for Homeland Defense Integration and Defense Support of Civil Authorities
- Joint Staff
  - J-3 Operations Directorate
  - J-5 Strategy, Policy, and Plans Directorate
- U.S. Northern Command (USNORTHCOM)
  - J-3 Operations Directorate
  - J-4 Logistics and Engineering Directorate
  - J-5 Strategy, Policy, and Plans Directorate
  - J-9 Interagency Directorate
- U.S. Pacific Command (USPACOM)
  - J-3 Operations Directorate
  - J-5 Strategic Planning and Policy
  - DCO/DCE Task Force East
- National Guard Bureau (NGB)
  - J-3 Domestic Operations Directorate
  - J-5 Strategic Plans and Policy Directorate
  - J-8 Resources and Assessment Directorate
- U.S. Army Staff
  - G-34/Office of Domestic Preparedness
- U.S. Army North (ARNORTH)
  - USNORTHCOM liaison officer
  - DCO/DCE Region II
  - DCO/DCE Region VII.

Finally, we conducted an in-depth analysis of FEMA's ten regional AHPs from the perspective of DoD support. To better appreciate how DoD might fit into these plans and the scenarios covered, we analyzed all the available AHPs to determine the specific threats addressed and the capabilities and resources earmarked for response efforts. Additionally, we looked at the roles and resources requested of DoD by each region as an initial step toward better synching the two organizations' concerted response to catastrophic events. Our purpose was not to compare the plans or evaluate their quality per se, but to assess whether they had sufficient information to allow the identification of gaps that might be filled by DoD capabilities. The information collected from our literature review, our interviews, and our analysis of FEMA's AHPs fed into the development of our recommendations for how to improve DoD support to FEMA.

Organization of This Report

Chapter Two presents our analysis of FEMA's AHPs and the potential capability gaps we identified. This chapter assesses each of the AHPs and identifies capabilities that the plans expect will be requested from DoD. The chapter also presents ways to improve interagency coordination with respect to the AHPs.

Chapter Three presents our analysis of DSCA as currently provided by DoD in support of FEMA regional plans, including a synopsis of DSCA planning at the operational level. This chapter also presents our findings from interviews with DoD stakeholders at various levels, from OSD and the Joint Staff to CCMD and DCOs and their DCEs.

Chapter Four presents our main conclusions and recommendations for improving DoD support to FEMA.

Appendix A provides background on national disaster planning and response by examining the various elements of the national approach to preparedness. It describes the main policies and plans that guide disaster response in the United States, then identifies the main disaster response mechanisms used at the local, state, and federal levels. It ends by providing an overview of FEMA authorities and responsibilities, as well as DoD authorities and responsibilities and their implications for DSCA.

Appendix B presents an overview of key policies and other DoD guidance on the conduct of DSCA.

CHAPTER TWO

Review of FEMA All-Hazards Plans and Identification of Potential Capability Gaps

Each of FEMA's ten regions is responsible for writing and updating comprehensive AHPs that guide response efforts in the wake of disasters, including large-scale catastrophes (see Figure 2.1). According to the U.S. Government Accountability Office (GAO), these plans, developed in conjunction with state and local authorities, form the backbone of the federal response to disasters and are intended to "inform DOD of the local and state-level capabilities available for responding to a complex catastrophe in each FEMA region, as well as any capability gaps that might ultimately have to be filled by DOD or another federal agency."[1]

Figure 2.1
Map of FEMA Regions

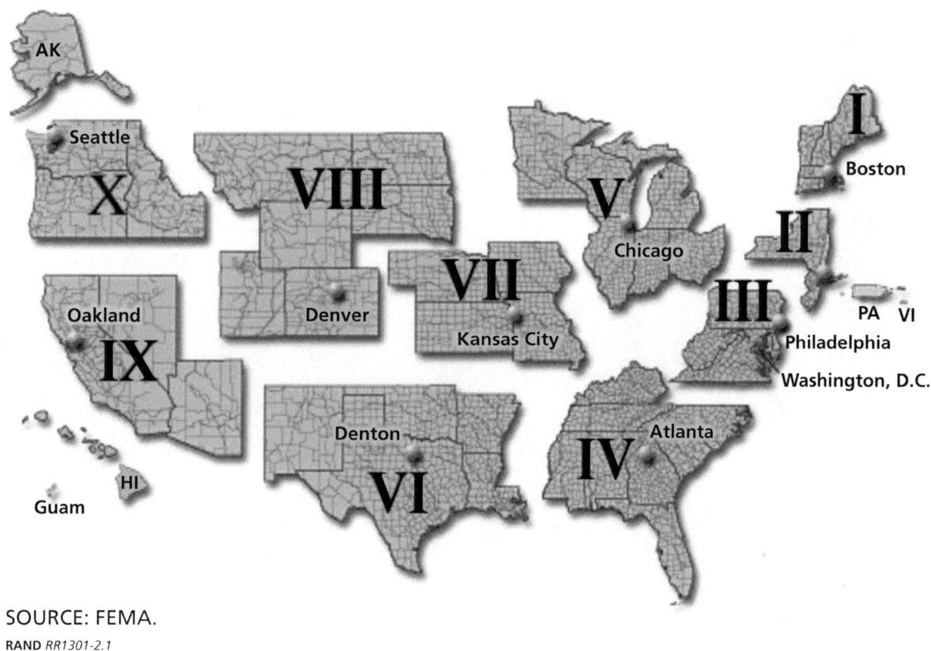

SOURCE: FEMA.
RAND RR1301-2.1

---

[1] U.S. Government Acountability Office, *Report to Congressional Requestors: Civil Support: Actions Are Needed to Improve DOD's Planning for a Complex Catastrophe*, Washington, D.C., GAO-13-763, September 2013, p. 12.

Analysis of FEMA All-Hazards Plans

The AHPs written and maintained by each of the ten FEMA regions represent a critical tool in coordinating efforts to respond to large-scale catastrophes throughout the United States and its territories. Several of these plans are highly detailed, thorough documents that enumerate specific actions, phased responses, and resources that will be called on in the event of such a catastrophe. There remains, however, considerable variation in the level of detail and specificity of the AHPs as regards threat analysis and DoD involvement. Because DoD is most likely to be called on in the event of a large-scale catastrophe, we have focused our analysis on these elements of planning and response.

Analytic Approach

The AHPs are intended to represent a standardized way for FEMA to plan for response operations in each of its ten regions.[2] To better appreciate how DoD might fit into these plans and the scenarios covered, we analyzed all of the available AHPs to determine the specific threats addressed and the capabilities and resources earmarked for response efforts. Additionally, we looked at the role and resources requested of DoD by each region as an initial step toward better synching the two organizations' concerted response to catastrophic events. Our purpose was not to compare the plans or evaluate their quality per se, but to assess whether they had sufficient information to allow the identification of gaps that might be filled by DoD capabilities. Table 2.1 provides a snapshot of the AHPs in their current iterations as available on FEMA's WebEOC portal.

Assessment of FEMA's All-Hazard Plans

Where complete and thorough, these AHPs offer essential guidance and information to DoD planners. They can use this specific guidance to prepare and plan for the type of capabilities that will be requested of them by FEMA or state and local authorities and designate specific resources and assets to these contingencies in the event of a disaster. In the regions where the AHPs lack specificity and threat assessments, it will be more difficult to plan accordingly, and DoD response may be less rapid and less targeted to the specific needs of the requesting agencies. Prior planning and coordination is the best way to ensure that civilian and DoD authorities are on the same page before a large-scale catastrophe occurs to ensure a more fluid, concerted joint response.

There is considerable overlap in the types of support capabilities requested of DoD by the ten FEMA regions. These requests relate to particular emergency support functions (ESFs)—which we discuss in Appendix A—and often represent complex logistical capabilities that the regions do not consider themselves capable of handling during a catastrophe without external support. The requested DoD capabilities most often fall under the following general categories:

- Transportation (ESF #1)
- Communications (ESF #2)
- Airlift and evacuation support (ESF #5)

[2] Several interviewees posited that one of the advantages of regional plans is that they provide a neutral means of recording capability gaps within states. The logic being that, if a state emergency management agency admits to having gaps, it would become a political issue in the next gubernatorial election (USNORTHCOM interviews, December 16, 2014; OSD interviews, February 5, 2015; DCE interviews, June 3, 2015).

Table 2.1
DoD Requirements in FEMA All-Hazards Plans

Region	Threat Analysis Included	Role of DoD Adequately Explained to Enable Planning	Specific DoD Resources/ Quantities Requested	Large-Scale Catastrophes Addressed	Overall Impression
I	Yes	Yes	Yes/Yes	Major threats and necessary responses thoroughly detailed	• Comprehensive list of plans and contingencies in each state • Contains an extensive tasking of DoD resources—specifically tasks roles and resources • Targeted response capabilities and expectations for disasters • Tailored to major catastrophes
II	Yes	Yes	Some	Somewhat—tsunami ISP for Puerto Rico/U.S. Virgin Islands in progress	• Reasonably thorough • Missing specific scenario plans
III	No	No	No/No	No	• Contains only sketches of responsibilities and divisions of task • No specific guidance for DoD
IV	Yes	Yes	Yes/No	No ISPs, but hurricanes and other threats directly addressed	• Comprehensive detailed plan of how to implement emergency protocol in every situation • State-by-state breakdown provides detailed information
V	Yes	Somewhat	Yes/No	No ISPs, but detailed fact sheet on major types of threats	• Detailed lists of phases and tasks (with similar checklists) • Limited concrete support tasks for DoD and little specificity for actions • Conducted major improvised nuclear device exercise in 2013
VI	Yes	Yes	Yes/Yes	No ISPs, but major threats directly addressed	• Detailed plan with specific threats and types/quantities of DoD resources specified • Clear expectations of DoD
VII	No	No	No/No	Detailed, specific New Madrid Seismic Zone Plan in place for Missouri but region-wide ISP still not available	• Plan barely addresses role of DoD • Few if any resources mentioned • Reviews ESFs but provides only broad information
VIII	Not Finalized/Not Available				

Table 2.1—Continued

Region	Threat Analysis Included	Role of DoD Adequately Explained to Enable Planning	Specific DoD Resources/ Quantities Requested	Large-Scale Catastrophes Addressed	Overall Impression
IX	Somewhat	No	No/No	Detailed, thorough ISPs for Southern California and Northern California earthquakes and tsunamis and Hawaii and Guam catastrophe plans	• Role of DoD (DCO/DCE) only vaguely mentioned in support capacity for broad missions • Lacks specificity
X	Somewhat	No	No/No	Somewhat—ISP in progress for Cascadia Subduction Zone earthquake	• Provides only a cursory sketch of roles and responsibilities with little information on task breakdowns, resources, or role of DoD

Key:

Thorough and complete; comprehensive plan.

Reasonably thorough and complete; some missing sections or information.

Not thorough or complete; missing a lot of information; lacks specificity.

- Search and rescue (SAR) (ESF #5)
- Logistics (ESF #7)
- Base installation support (ESF #7)
- Mass care/medical support (ESF #8)
- Mass fatality management (ESF #8).

This list echoes the perspectives of FEMA personnel who indicated that DoD could provide several key capabilities, depending on the incident. These include[3]

- mass fatality management
- personnel
- CBRN response
- airlift
- reestablishing the electrical grid/power restoration support.

In addition to the AHPs, several regions have also written or are currently writing incident-specific plans (ISPs), which highlight particular dangers and scenarios endemic to the region. These ISPs provide detailed responses for large-scale catastrophes, including earthquakes in Region VII (New Madrid Seismic Zone), Region IX (in Northern and Southern California), and Region X (Cascadia Subduction Zone—plan in progress), as well as tsunamis in Region II (Puerto Rico and the U.S. Virgin Islands—plan in progress) and a Region IX catastrophic plan for Hawaii and Guam. These plans offer specific, tailored guidance for the most likely, high-level threats that each region faces. The Southern and Northern California earthquake

[3] Interviews with FEMA officials, February 26, 2015, and April 24, 2015.

plans, the Hawaii catastrophic hurricane plan, and the Guam catastrophe plan (the only ones currently available) provide a detailed accounting of exactly how state and local authorities will respond in the event of an earthquake or other catastrophic event and list specific FEMA and DoD resources that would be needed if an incident were to befall any of these areas. An ISP for an improvised nuclear device or a similar mass casualty event for major urban centers has been discussed but has yet to be written.

Recommendations to Improve FEMA Plans

From on our review of these plans, as well as our wider review of the disaster preparedness literature and our interviews with subject-matter experts, we identified the following recommendations.

Clear expectations for types and numbers of resources are critical for DoD to be able to fully support FEMA in the wake of a disaster, particularly a large-scale catastrophe. DoD and FEMA should consider ways to identify remaining information gaps and ways to close them, as well as ways to make expectations on both sides more explicit and understood. While requests are submitted from FEMA to DoD in the form of capabilities, it would help DoD planners to know what specific resources might be needed or expected, while still affording DoD flexibility and discretion in response. The AHPs should reference the need for specific capabilities in the form of approximate numbers (e.g., weights, distances, personnel) that might be requested by the FEMA regions, with the understanding that these would be rough estimates for planning purposes.[4]

Additionally, DoD (and other agencies involved in disaster response) would benefit from a listing of specific actions and capabilities that are likely to be requested in response to large-scale catastrophes. In most regions, FEMA has solid procedures and checklists in place. However, it is not clear where the additional resources and assets (both materiel and personnel) to implement these plans will come from in the event of a catastrophe. Identification of resources should improve DoD planning, which in turn would enable a faster response. The ISPs that do exist are comprehensive in identifying requirements for DoD and could be used as exemplars. Several other region-specific ISPs are still in progress or unavailable. These plans will provide key guidance in the event of a catastrophe, so DoD might wish to identify opportunities to facilitate their development.

Utilization of FEMA's regional plans in planning and exercising is not as extensive as it could be, and this issue may cause delays in response activities. DoD and other stakeholders are sometimes unaware of the contents of these plans and have not taken the steps necessary to gain access to them. Widespread DoD access to the AHPs and ISPs is essential for effective and timely response; DoD should work with FEMA to ensure that every relevant response unit and branch has direct access to these plans or knows how to access them.[5] Even with DoD support, it took us several weeks to gain web access to the AHPs. And even with full access to FEMA's WebEOC portal, the website does not currently have all ten AHPs, and the material it does have is not well organized. The Region VIII plan is not available, and the Region X plan, though it is available through a general Internet search, is not on the site. Additionally, there is

---

[4] For example, there would be such language as "vertical lift capability sufficient for mass casualty transport of 1,000 people." The AHPs should not request specific items of equipment, such as "12 V-22 or Blackhawks."

[5] Although outside the scope of this effort, it would likely also be valuable for DoD to share with FEMA, in a manner consistent with its security requirements, any plans that it develops for supporting AHPs and ISPs.

only one ISP (Guam) housed on the site. This portal represents a potentially useful tool to share FEMA's plans in a controlled environment, but it should be publicized and made more readily available and user-friendly to the broader array of DoD users as well as the civilian response community.[6]

---

[6] Some of our DoD interviewees indicated to us that they do not have access to the FEMA AHPs.

CHAPTER THREE

Review of Policies, Plans, and Procedures for Defense Support of Civil Authorities Provided to FEMA by DoD

Introduction

Focusing on FEMA's regional AHPs, this chapter presents our analysis of DSCA policies, plans, and procedures for providing DoD support to FEMA. We do not include support to civilian law enforcement agencies, wildland firefighting support to the National Interagency Fire Center, national special security events, or nonemergency support provided under the provisions of the Economy Act (31 U.S.C. 1535), as these activities are beyond the scope of this report.[1] Additionally, we consider only the employment of federal military forces in a Title 10 status under the command of the president. We assume the National Guard is a state asset unless federalized under Title 10, as illustrated in the right third of the box in Figure 3.1.[2]

In addition to the assessment of FEMA plans and processes presented in Chapter Two, we conducted this analysis by reviewing DoD guidance, Joint Staff orders, key CCMD plans, and external reports, such as those by GAO and the Congressional Research Service. A detailed list of the relevant policies and guidance reviewed can be found in Appendix B. Finally, and perhaps most importantly, we interviewed more than two dozen military officers and civilian officials assigned to key stakeholder offices and units.

This chapter presents a synopsis of DSCA planning at the operational level, as well as findings in the form of best practices and challenges, from interviews with DoD stakeholders at various levels from OSD and the Joint Staff to CCMD and DCOs/DCEs. It is focused on how DoD policy, plans, and procedures might be changed to improve support to FEMA. The resulting analysis supports the conclusions and recommendations found in Chapter Four.

---

[1] Although aspects of DSCA, these activities fall outside DoD support to FEMA's AHPs.

[2] Doctrine, policy, and historical experience indicate that National Guard assets will in the vast majority of cases be employed in response to the incident prior to the request for assistance from federal military forces and normally operate under the command of the governor either on state active duty or under U.S. Code, Title 32. See Joint Publication (JP) 3-28, *Defense Support of Civil Authorities*, Washington, D.C.: Joint Chiefs of Staff, July 2013, pp. I-6, II-2 through II-5, and Appendix D; and Army Doctrine Reference Publication (ADRP) 3-28, *Defense Support of Civil Authorities*, Washington, D.C.: Department of the Army, June 2013, pp. II-8 and II-9, for discussion of various authorities for use of National Guard forces for DSCA. Except for certain niche capabilities, federal military forces should not be requested unless the necessary response to the incident exceeds the capacity of the National Guard. We briefly address dual-status commanders (DSC) in a later section.

Figure 3.1
Range of Response

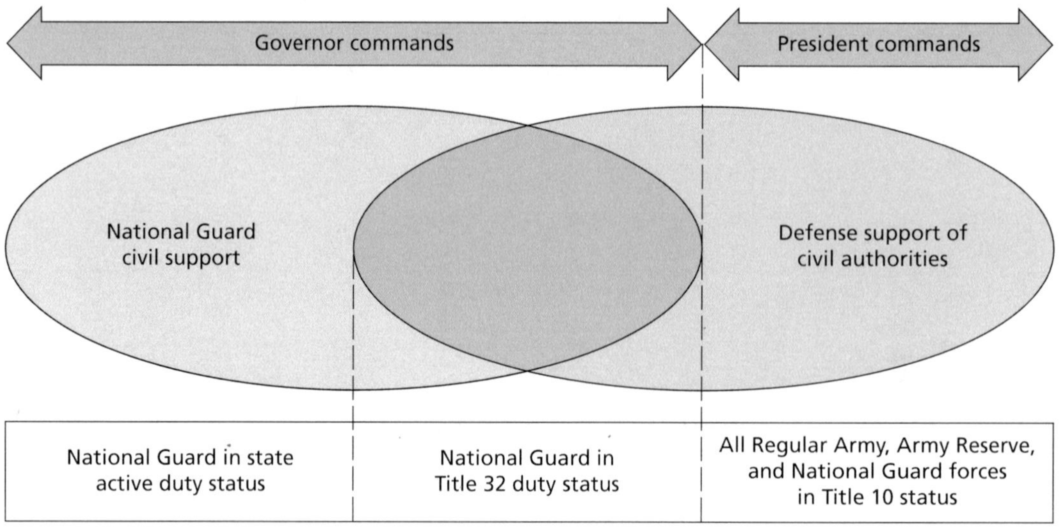

SOURCE: ADRP 3-28, 2013, p. 1-22.
RAND *RR1301-3.1*

Combatant Command Planning

DoD Directive (DoDD) 3025.18 assigns the following tasks, among others, to CCMDs with DSCA responsibilities:[3]

- Plan and execute DSCA operations in their areas of responsibility.
- Incorporate DSCA into joint training and exercise programs.
- Advocate for needed DSCA capabilities and requirements through the Joint Requirements Oversight Council.

According to JP 3-28, the supported geographic commanders for DSCA are USNORTHCOM and USPACOM. They "are DOD's principal planning agents for DSCA, and have the responsibility to provide joint planning and execution directives for peacetime assistance rendered by DOD within their assigned areas of responsibility (AOR)."[4] Additionally, the Joint Staff has issued various planning orders (PLANORDs) and standing execution orders (EXORDs). A recent PLANORD directs USNORTHCOM and USPACOM to develop plans for the conduct of DSCA operations and to initiate certain actions should a complex catastrophe occur. The EXORDs provide USNORTHCOM and USPACOM authorities and resources to conduct certain DSCA activities.[5]

---

[3] DoDD 3025.18, *Defense Support of Civil Authorities (DSCA)*, Washington, D.C., September 21, 2012, p. 13.

[4] JP 3-28, 2013, pp. II-7 and II-14. Detailed CCMD responsibilities are formally assigned through the Unified Command Plan, a classified document approved by the president.

[5] Joint Staff interviews, October 24, 2014; NGB interviews, November 5, 2014; USNORTHCOM interviews, December 16, 2014; OSD interviews, November 24, 2014, and February 5, 2015; and USPACOM interviews, March 26, 2015.

The primary CCMD-level plans for carrying out DSCA operations are Concpet of Operations Plan (CONPLAN) 3500-14, issued by USNORTHCOM, and CONPLAN 5001, issued by USPACOM.[6] They each provide a framework for DSCA operations within their respective AORs. Consistent with the doctrine published in JP 3-28, these plans are compatible with the NRF and the National Incident Management System (NIMS), as illustrated in Figure 3.2, and were developed in coordination with the relevant civilian emergency planners.[7]

Both CONPLAN 3500-14 and CONPLAN 5001 provide a basis for federal military response operations ranging from requests for assistance that require relatively few DoD assets to complex catastrophes that would require many thousands of federal military personnel and vast quantities of logistics support. However, the two CCMDs take different approaches to their respective CONPLANs. This should not be surprising, since USNORTHCOM and USPACOM have considerably different sets of geography in their AORs. The solid land masses of the continental United States and Alaska form the bulk of the USNORTHCOM AOR, while the USPACOM AOR for DSCA consists of archipelagos (Figure 3.3). Although

Figure 3.2
National Incident Management System Framework

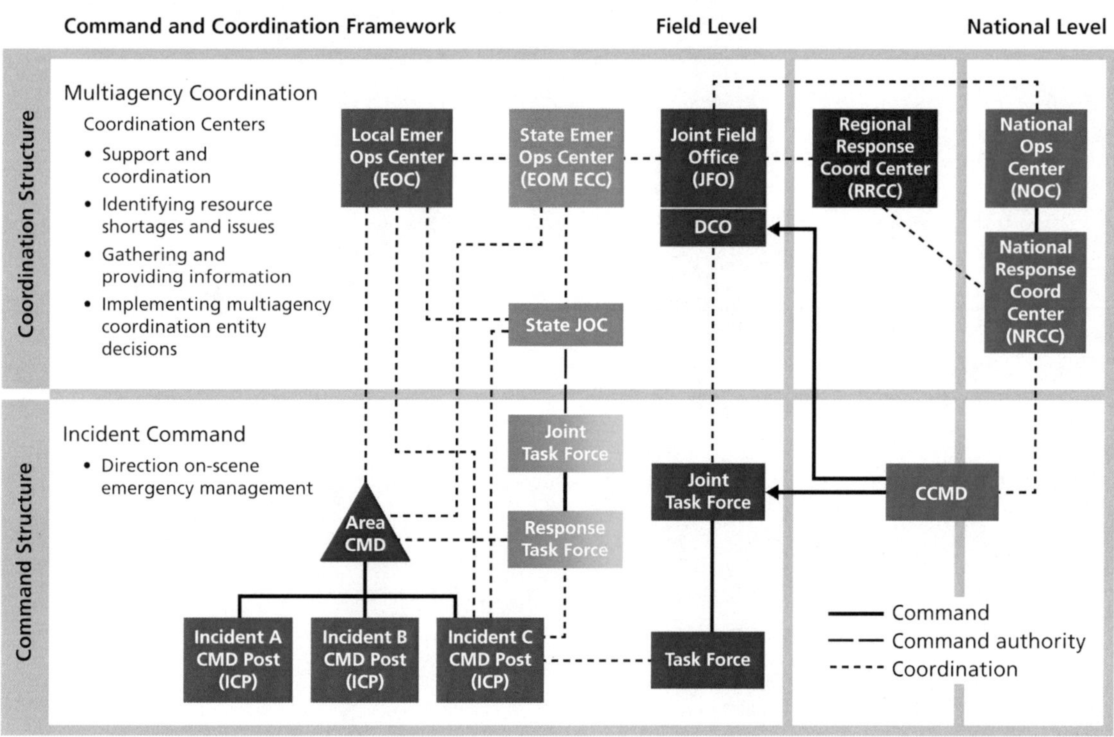

SOURCE: DoD, *DSCA Handbook: Tactical Level Commander and Staff Toolkit*, Washington D.C., GTA 90-01-020, July 2010a, p. 2-4.
RR1301-3.2

6 These documents are not available to the general public.

7 JP 3-26, *Defense Support of Civil Authorities*, Washington, D.C.: Joint Chiefs of Staff, July 31, 2013, pp. II-11 and II-14. Also, USNORTHCOM interviews, December 16, 2014; OSD interviews February 5, 2015; and USPACOM interviews, March 26, 2015.

Figure 3.3
USPACOM DSCA Joint Operating Area

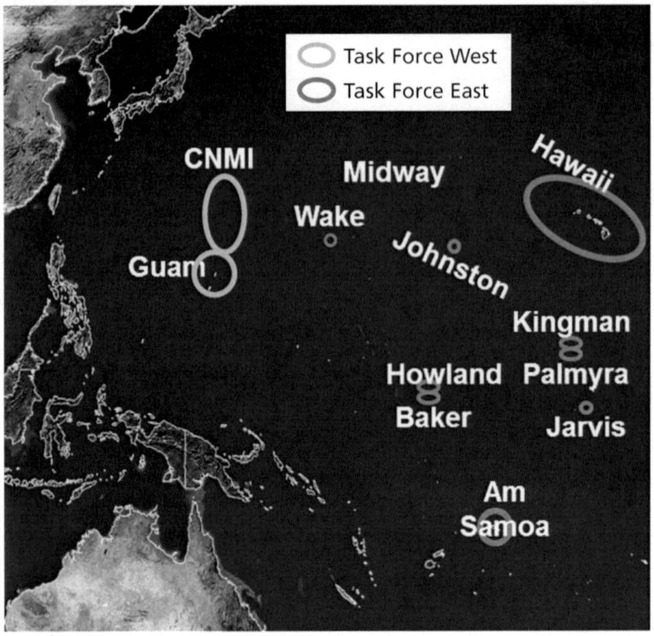

SOURCE: USPACOM J33.
NOTE: CNMI = Commonwealth of the Northern Mariana Islands.
RAND *RR1301-3.3*

USPACOM is responsible for a much smaller portion of the U.S. landmass, the size of its total AOR is several times that of USNORTHCOM's.

Furthermore, homeland defense, DSCA, and security cooperation are the primary missions of USNORTHCOM and nearly the sole focus of its commander. USPACOM, however, devotes most of its planning to regional cooperation and preparing for wartime contingencies. USPACOM also has greater responsibilities to plan for foreign disaster relief/humanitarian assistance operations and works with the Office of Foreign Disaster Assistance (OFDA) in a manner similar to its planning and coordination with FEMA. In September 2009, for example, USPACOM supported FEMA for DSCA in American Samoa at the same time it was supporting OFDA with foreign disaster relief in the Philippines and shortly thereafter in Thailand.[8]

Within CONPLAN 3500-14, USNORTHCOM developed an overarching complex catastrophe branch plan concept of operations that identifies initial actions to be taken by the CCMD and subordinate elements. This concept of operations is supported by a series of what USNORTHCOM calls "playbooks" that identify the key elements of the federal military response to various types of complex catastrophes. They are roughly equivalent to course of action sketches used in the military decisionmaking process.[9] The playbooks are

---

[8] USPACOM interviews, March 26, 2015.

[9] See ADRP 1-02, *Terms and Military Symbols*, Washington, D.C.: Department of the Army, February 2015, Chapter 10; and JP 5-0, *Joint Operation Planning*, Washington, D.C.: Joint Chiefs of Staff, August 11, 2011, pp. IV-17 through IV-43.

USNORTHCOM-specific but will form the basis for integrated USNORTHCOM regional supporting plans that support FEMA region ISPs.[10]

The USPACOM approach to planning for complex catastrophes was to develop a single complex catastrophe scenario within its CONPLAN. This scenario will be the basis for contingency operations in response to a particular disaster, should one occur. USPACOM planners stated that, because of the nature of its AOR and that it has assigned forces, "USPACOM doesn't need several specific scenarios as would be suitable for a multi-state disaster in CONUS [continental United States]."[11] USPACOM did not use the intermediate step of creating playbooks but instead wrote a single DSCA contingency operations plan, which it can pivot from depending on the situation.

The USNORTHCOM CONPLAN is a work in progress, because additional scenarios to address certain types of catastrophes in specific regions are being developed in coordination with civilian emergency planners and then added to the plans. For example, USNORTHCOM is currently developing several playbooks, such as one for an earthquake in the New Madrid Seismic Zone that would affect FEMA Regions IV, V, VI, and VII. It is also developing regional supporting plans that include an earthquake in the Cascadia Subduction Zone (Regions IX and X). USNORTHCOM has established a prioritized list for developing approximately 30 additional playbooks and regional support plans by 2020.[12]

Defense Coordinating Officers/Defense Coordinating Elements

DCOs are Regular Army colonels assigned to each FEMA region.[13] The single DoD point of contact in the Joint Field Office after a catastrophe takes place, DCOs are the linchpins for federal military force coordination with the FEMA regions. They also play a critical role in supporting FEMA regional planning. Most, if not all, participate in both FEMA region and state emergency management agency exercises.[14] They also work closely with state National Guards to provide expertise on federal military roles and visibility on state National Guard planning.[15] Except in Region IX, where the DCOs for Hawaii and Guam are assigned to USPACOM, they are assigned to ARNORTH, a subordinate command of USNORTHCOM. The rater for their annual officer evaluation reports is the ARNORTH deputy commanding general, and the senior rater is the ARNORTH commanding general.[16]

Additionally, due to the distances from the portion of FEMA Region IX to the mainland, USPACOM has two additional DCOs. DCO West has responsibility for DSCA in Guam and

---

[10] Region ISPs are part of each region's AHPs.

[11] USPACOM interviews, March 26, 2015.

[12] USNORTHCOM interviews, December 16, 2014.

[13] Except for Region IX, in which Guam's DCO is a Navy flag officer who has delegated the responsibilities to a Navy civilian.

[14] In interviews and all the cases we observed, this was the case, but we did not confirm with every DCO.

[15] DCE email, June 8, 2015. By "visibility on state National Guard planning," we mean that the DCO is aware of state plans within his or her region, participates in exercises involving state National Guard resources, and provides linkage between state National Guard and CCMD plans.

[16] DCE interviews, June 3, 2015. The DCO for Hawaii is rated by the 8th Theater Sustainment Command. The DCO for Guam is rated by the commander of Naval Forces Marianas.

the Commonwealth of the Northern Mariana Islands. DCO East has responsibility for DSCA in the Hawaiian Islands and American Samoa.[17] They work in close coordination with the ARNORTH FEMA Region IX DCO.[18]

DCEs support the DCO and essentially function as his or her staff. In the case of larger disasters, the DCE may be augmented with additional staff, as illustrated in Figure 3.4.

For both USNORTHCOM and USPACOM, the DCOs play a key role in supporting FEMA regional planning by identifying how DoD capabilities can assist, including the routine identification of gaps in FEMA regional plans and feeding that information to USNORTHCOM and USPACOM planners. They accomplish this through participation in FEMA planning forums, exercises, and discussions with CCMD staffs.[19]

Both USNORTHCOM and USPACOM interviewees posited that, in many cases, the DCEs are currently understaffed, given the need (but not necessarily an official "requirement" in DoD terms) to support FEMA regional planning.[20] One interviewee stated that the original construct was for the DCE to consist of 25 to 30 staff from multiple services, but instead, the

Figure 3.4
Example of Defense Coordinating Element Organization

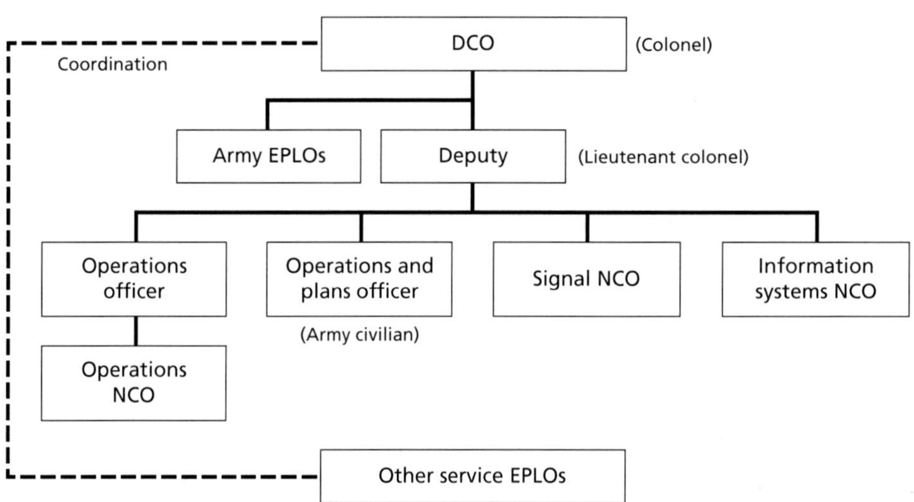

SOURCE: ADRP 3-28, 2013, p. 3-3.
NOTES: EPLO = emergency preparedness liaison officer. NCO = noncommissioned officer.
RAND *RR1301-3.4*

---

[17] Email from PACOM J33/Homeland Defense, June 5, 2015.

[18] USPACOM interviews, March 19, 2015, and March 26, 2015.

[19] USNORTHCOM and ARNORTH interviews, December 16, 2014; USPACOM interviews, March 26, 2015; OSD interviews, November 24, 2014, and February 5, 2015; DCE interviews, June 3, 2015. Also see Joseph W. Kirschbaum, *Civil Support: DOD Is Taking Action to Strengthen Support of Civil Authorities*, testimony before the Subcommittee on Emergency Preparedness, Response, and Communications, Committee on Homeland Security, House of Representatives, Washington, D.C.: U.S. Government Accountability Office, GAO-15-686T, June 10, 2015, p 10.

[20] FEMA interviewees also stated the DCEs, in many cases, were not adequately staffed (FEMA interviews, April 24, 2015). We also note that the GAO has reported that DCE staffing is not based upon a needs assessment (GAO, *DOD Can Enhance Efforts to Identify Capabilities to Support Civil Authorities During Disasters*, Washington, D.C., GAO 10-386, March 2010, p. 37). Given the variation in frequency of disasters and the risk of catastrophic events between the regions, authorizing roughly the same DCE staffing for all regions may not adequately match the requirements to the authorizations.

permanent staff is typically 11 or 12 persons (of whom two are civilians and either nine or ten are military personnel), all from the Army.[21] However, when we interviewed personnel from three different DCEs, they reported that they believed their DCEs were appropriately sized, given that their respective FEMA regions used outside contractors to write the majority of their regional AHPs and did not request or require DCE assistance in developing the civilian aspects of the FEMA regional plans.[22]

However, DCOs/DCEs did express concern regarding their relationship with ARNORTH in terms of their authorities for administrative issues, such as approving temporary duty, as well as not being a joint organization.[23] Given that we interviewed members of only three out of 12 DCEs (counting the two additional USPACOM DCEs), we were not able to adequately assess the sufficiency of DCE staffing but suggest that OSD may wish to consider this issue as it develops a new DoD instruction to address DSCA liaison arrangements.

Military emergency preparedness liaison officers (EPLOs) are senior reserve component officers authorized in each FEMA region and each state. They are managed by and under the control of their respective services until activated. Nonetheless, they can support the DCOs during preincident planning ("Phase 0"). Upon activation following a catastrophe, they come under operational control of the supported CCMD (either USNORTHCOM or USPACOM), who will place them under tactical control of the DCO.[24]

During the FEMA Trade Winds Exercise in June 2015, we observed that the DCE had been augmented by a U.S. Army Reserve Command civil military planning officer (who is a full-time Department of the Army civilian), two U.S. Marine Corps EPLOs, and an Army EPLO, who were colocated with the DCE at the FEMA Regional Command Center. The DCE reported that additional liaison officers were located with the DCE forward element in the U.S. Virgin Islands. At least in this instance, the observation validated the availability of EPLOs to participate in Phase 0 activities despite being under control of their service, rather than the DCO.

Stakeholder Perceptions

To help assess how DoD support to FEMA regional planning might be improved, we interviewed more than two dozen military officers and civilian officials assigned to OSD, the Joint Staff, USNORTHCOM, USPACOM, NGB, ARNORTH, Army G3/Western Hemisphere Emergency Management (WHEM; formerly Directorate of Military Support—DOMS), two DCOs and members of three different DCEs, a former National Guard Civil Support Team commander, and observed DCE-FEMA Region staff interactions during the Trade Winds Hurricane Exercise. We used a nonrandom convenience sample based on recommendations of

---

[21] Most DCEs have 11 persons, but a few with remote area responsibilities—such as the U.S. Virgin Islands for the FEMA Region II DCE—have 12. USNORTHCOM and ARNORTH interviews, December 16, 2014; USPACOM interviews, March 26, 2015; DCE interviews, June 3, 2015.

[22] Although beyond the scope of this study, it could be argued that an inclusive planning process that was less dependent on contractual assistance would be inherently beneficial to all parties.

[23] DCE interviews June 3, 2015.

[24] DoD, 2010a, p. 3-15; and JP 3-28, 2012, pp. II-13 and II-14. The Joint Staff DSCA EXORD designates specific command relationships.

the sponsor, our assessment of which DoD organizations are key to DSCA processes, recommendations of interviewees, and the availability of personnel. The interviews were conducted under rules of nonattribution, approximately half individually and half in focus group sessions.

Although there is some overlap between categories, the next section is organized by topic under the headings of best practices and challenges.

Best Practices in DSCA Support to FEMA

Our assessment—shared by many of the stakeholders we interviewed—is that DoD support to FEMA regional planning is working well in some areas, and in these cases DoD should consider sustaining and even building on them. This is not an all-inclusive list, but highlights areas that were particularly notable during interviews and other research into current plans and recent exercise experiences.

Integration with FEMA Planning

Interviewees from both CCMDs stated that interagency coordination and planning was a significant aspect of their missions. They have exchanged liaison officers with FEMA headquarters and have staff directorates that are specifically dedicated to interagency coordination.

USNORTHCOM and USPACOM are integrated with FEMA regional planning through both the DCO for each region and through additional support from the CCMD planning staffs. Both have robust CONPLANS for DSCA, with several scenarios/playbooks already completed and, in the case of USNORTHCOM, many others in development. USNORTHCOM in particular recognizes this as one of its primary missions. In most cases, the DCOs have limited planning capability,[25] and USNORTHCOM planners have identified key scenarios for which USNORTHCOM planners will develop playbooks and FEMA region support plans. Military interviewees consistently stated that DCOs and CCMD planning staffs attend FEMA regional planning forums and participate in multiple exercises. USNORTHCOM and USPACOM have identified gaps in some FEMA regional plans and have established milestones to develop additional plans to provide DoD capabilities where needed.

Nonetheless, FEMA officials stated they were not sufficiently informed regarding the details in the USNORTHCOM playbooks. They felt the playbooks should provide more details regarding capabilities, resources, and authorities. FEMA interviewees also indicated they desired to have a better understanding of DoD command-and-control arrangements between DCOs and joint task force commanders at a disaster site and DoD leadership in the Pentagon.[26] DoD should consider ways to improve information sharing and coordination between DoD planning and FEMA planning, and ways to improve interagency understanding of DoD command and control arrangements.

USNORTHCOM and USPACOM, and particularly their DCOs, coordinate closely with the National Guard, primarily at the state level, viewing the National Guard as a state

[25] The perception of DCOs/DCEs having a limited planning capability was expressed at the CCMD level (USNORTHCOM interviews, December 16, 2014; USPACOM interviews, March 26, 2015) and reported in GAO, 2010, p. 37. However, as noted previously, the DCE personnel we interviewed stated their planning capabilities were adequate. We did not try to resolve the difference in perspectives, but speculate that it may be due to CCMD staff taking up the slack through their own support to FEMA regional planning.

[26] FEMA interviews, April 24, 2015. It was unclear from out interviews whether this was a communications shortfall between DoD and FEMA, or between FEMA headquarters and FEMA regions. This may be an area where the CCMDs, Joint Staff, or OSD could improve the socialization of DSCA plans with FEMA headquarters.

capability despite being military forces. Plans for the use of federal military forces consider the provision of niche capabilities or adding capacity if the National Guard—including through the use of the Emergency Management Assistance Compact (EMAC)—cannot adequately meet the requests for assistance from civilian authorities.[27]

Several FEMA officials, however, indicated that they need a better understanding of what capabilities states possess through EMAC so FEMA can assist other states (the states, they said, understand each other's capabilities very well).[28] They reported that EMAC works very well for the states and help with the movement of National Guard and other emergency response assets, but it is also important for FEMA and DoD to understand what National Guard and other state resources are available to ensure awareness of state military capabilities that may need to be reinforced by DoD.[29]

DCOs and DCE personnel with planning responsibility receive several weeks of training on DSCA planning, including courses conducted by ARNORTH and by FEMA. DCE military personnel stated they had developed sufficient knowledge, if not expertise, in DSCA processes and disaster response planning through such training. The two DCE civilian personnel we interviewed reported they had each been in their positions approximately ten years, after retiring from military careers, and could claim expertise in DSCA operations and planning. The civilian personnel help provide continuity, while each soldier rotates to another assignment after approximately three years.

Several interviewees reported the perception that DCO/DCE relationships with FEMA region personnel vary depending upon the personalities of the DCO and his or her FEMA region administrator as well as the size of the regional headquarters and the frequency of disasters within the region. In most cases, they reported that the DCO feels like a fully integrated member of the region administrator's staff whose advice is sought and is routinely brought into planning and decisionmaking forums. In other cases, it was reported that relationships were perceived as cordial but "we will call you when we need you" in character.[30]

DoD should consider sustaining the best practice of integrating DoD planning with FEMA planning at the regional level, including use of CCMD staffs and DCO/DCEs.[31] These processes might be institutionalized in the new instruction being developed to address liaison issues (DoDI 3025.jj). Additionally, DoD should consider performing an assessment of the current size and composition of the DCEs and consider making them joint and increasing the number of personnel assigned to FEMA regions that are assessed as having greater risk of a complex catastrophe.

Logistics Support Planning

USNORTHCOM's J4 Mobility Division works closely with FEMA to get advance notice if it appears likely that strategic airlift will be needed. The Interagency Transportation Support

---

[27] USNORTHCOM interviews, December 16, 2014; NGB interviews, November 5, 2014; USPACOM interviews, March 26, 2015; and G3/WHEM interviews, April 16, 2015. EMAC is an interstate agreement to facilitate sharing of state emergency response resources, including National Guard forces, between states. See Appendix A for additional details.

[28] An assessment of the states' understanding of one another's capabilities was outside of the scope of this report.

[29] FEMA interviews, April 24, 2015.

[30] USNORTHCOM interviews, December 16, 2014; DCE interviews, June 3, 2015.

[31] This also requires collaboration on the part of FEMA, for example, by explicitly requesting and encouraging substantive DCO/DCE participation in the planning process.

Framework concept of operations was developed to ensure FEMA crisis response teams are properly trained on preparing their cargo for movement on DoD aircraft. FEMA personnel are trained on a space available basis at DoD installations on pallet buildup, hazardous material documentation, and cargo load plans. Initiatives described in CONPLAN 3500-14 to make support available more quickly include building a database with weight and cubic feet for various federal time-phased force and deployment lists.[32] A USNORTHCOM J4 Mobility Division movement control group is also working with FEMA to create a national-level and/or regional movement control group concept or standard operating procedure that would examine how deliveries into a disaster area should be prioritized. The usual military approach is a push system, which focuses on pushing forces, food, water, etc., into a disaster area, on the assumption that it is better to get responders and materials in place quickly and in large numbers, rather than using up valuable time to determine the exact needs. DoD is encouraging FEMA to develop a pull system, however, after the experience of ports of debarkation being overwhelmed during Hurricanes Katrina and Sandy. For example, according to one interviewee, "during the Hurricane Katrina response, so much water was delivered it overwhelmed reception capacity and crowded out other requirements."[33] Although outside the scope of this report, there is some evidence that FEMA is explicitly attempting to develop a push system. The USNORTHCOM J4 has been working with FEMA headquarters on the use of such programs as its contract with American Medical Response for air ambulance patient movement support in Region VI. USNORTHCOM mobility logistics planners reported that they are looking at how to increase what can be moved by FEMA contracted civilian assets and how DoD capabilities might fill the delta.

The USNORTHCOM Joint Logistics Operations Center supports the FEMA national logistics coordinator. Its current priorities are to (1) identify what may be needed and coordinate with the services and (2) plan for the DoD response to be self-sustaining. The center is also developing an installation usage guide that addresses logistics functional capabilities and helps choose base support installations and identify conflicts in demand between base support installations and federal staging areas.[34] Bringing stakeholders together, such as the National Guard, federal reserve components, and FEMA, the center discovered that many stakeholders had planned to use the same bases and would have exceeded their capacity in the event of a major disaster. The USNORTHCOM J4 approach is to give FEMA requirements priority and then deconflict National Guard and federal military force demands and to document National Guard plans for life support areas.[35]

DoD should consider sustaining the best practice of providing logistics support planning to FEMA to help identify what strategic lift and other transportation and material needs FEMA is likely to request after a catastrophe and to deconflict DoD, National Guard, and FEMA staging area plans to use DoD installations. Such efforts will improve the speed and efficiency of DSCA activities. USNORTHCOM should consider ways to do more to social-

[32] These lists identify the units or types of units required to support a CONPLAN or operations plan and when they are required to arrive.

[33] USNORTHCOM interviews, December 16, 2014.

[34] Base support installations are locations designated for DoD forces to perform reception, staging, onward movement, and integration. Federal staging areas are locations where civilian responders plan to conduct staging activities.

[35] USNORTHCOM interviews, December 16, 2014.

ize these plans with FEMA and other parts of the civilian response community, potentially including state and local governments, which may drive logistical needs but may also have facilities and other resources to contribute.

DoD Participation in FEMA Exercises

USNORTHCOM, USPACOM, and their DCOs routinely participate in FEMA exercises at the regional level, and the DCOs often participate in state-level exercises. Lessons from such participation are used to refine CCMD DSCA plans. For example, as a result of lessons from Ardent Sentry 14, NORTHCOM J4 is emphasizing Region X because of the logistic constraints in Alaska. One interviewee stated: "If Elmendorf AFB is the only airfield standing, throughput would be limited to 17 C-17s sorties per day, but it was discovered that FEMA, National Guard, and federal military forces had planned for far more airlift than could be supported by airfield capacity."

DoD should consider sustaining the best practice of participating in FEMA and state-level exercises to improve DoD DSCA plans and to enhance civilian responder awareness of DoD capabilities. This is primarily a CCMD responsibility, but OSD may wish to incorporate these activities into a DoD directive. However, as will be discussed below, the design of exercises might be improved in order to meet both DoD and FEMA objectives.

Key Challenges in DSCA Support to FEMA

DoD support to FEMA regional planning could be improved by resolving differences in perceptions about processes and time required to source forces for DSCA, resolving differences between DoD and FEMA planners regarding exercise objectives, testing the viability of active component (Title 10) dual-status commander during a multistate complex catastrophe, and improving CCMD visibility of unit and service immediate response activities. Our observations and analyses on these topics have implications for changes in DoD processes, policies, and/or authorities.

Conflicting Perceptions Within DoD of the Relative Priority of DSCA

Interviews indicated that different DoD organizations had different perceptions regarding the priority of DSCA versus warfighting.[36] These differences may be resolved by the recent publication of the 2015 National Military Strategy, which lists DSCA as number 11 out of the 12 joint force prioritized missions.[37] However, DSCA is still a priority mission, and there are differences regarding the implications of that prioritization. For example, interviewees assigned to the Joint Staff emphasized that[38]

- DoD does not recognize requirements specifically for DSCA.
- DoD does not and should not design or create capabilities specifically for DSCA.
- DoD should avoid being too proactive, "if DoD leans forward, civilian agencies will want to use it as 'The Easy Button' instead of developing their own capabilities."

---

[36] We describe the disparities we found between the viewpoints of various parts of DoD on this topic because it potentially affects DoD support to FEMA. These differences were not only notable during interviews but also apparent in "competing" comments provided by DoD stakeholders on an earlier draft of this report. Adjudicating these conflicts, however, is beyond the scope of this report.

[37] Joint Chiefs of Staff, *The National Military Strategy of the United States of America*, Washington, D.C., 2015.

[38] Joint Staff interviews, October 24, 2014, November 7, 2014, and November 19, 2014.

- Each ESF lead agency should be responsible for identifying capabilities and requirements for its respective ESF.
- Other federal agencies should carry out the lead for their ESFs before DoD jumps into the process by assisting with planning.

Regarding support to FEMA regional planning, some Joint Staff interviewees reported that, in most cases, DoD has already identified its capabilities for catastrophic incidents. For the scenarios that are exceptions, they stated that DoD should wait for FEMA to complete its own ongoing planning before providing planning assistance. They posited that a massive catastrophe, such as inundation from a tsunami caused by an earthquake in the Cascadia Subduction Zone, would be disastrous, but because it has a very low probability in the next three to five years, "we can afford to have strategic patience."[39]

Interviewees at OSD and USNORTHCOM, however, disputed the idea that DSCA is a secondary mission. While acknowledging that DoD capabilities for DSCA should be dual-use and acquired for warfighting requirements, they argued that DoD's *Strategy for Homeland Defense and Defense Support of Civil Authorities* and a 2012 Secretary of Defense memorandum titled "Actions to Improve Defense Support in Complex Catastrophes" provide clear guidance that DSCA is a high priority.[40]

It might be argued that this disparity is an example of the aphorism, "Where you stand depends on where you sit."[41] On the one hand, senior officials in OSD and at USNORTHCOM and USPACOM are the people most likely to be called to account if the DoD response to a disaster is perceived as being too slow. On the other hand, Joint Staff officers tend to be focused on managing organizational processes and conserving resources for warfighting. Nonetheless, we suggest there might be ambiguity in the current guidance, which is spread across several different documents that were published over a period of three years.

The *Strategy for Homeland Defense and Defense Support of Civil Authorities* states that DSCA is "one of the Department's primary missions"; a Secretary of Defense memorandum dated May 23, 2013, and titled "Planning to Support the Department of Homeland Security" directs that "DoD will establish a framework for all-hazards, Total Force, regional planning to integrate and coordinate, as appropriate, State National Guard and be integrated with, the Federal Emergency Management Agency's (FEMA) multi-year regional all-hazards and region scenario-specific planning efforts,"[42] and the 2014 Quadrennial Defense Review (QDR) states that "Protection of the homeland will also include sustaining capabilities to assist U.S. civil authorities in protecting U.S. airspace, shores, and borders, and in responding effectively to domestic man-made and natural disasters."[43] But the Chairman's Assessment of the 2014 QDR

---

[39] Joint Staff interviews, November 19, 2014.

[40] DoD, *Strategy for Homeland Defense and Defense Support of Civil Authorities*, Washington, D.C., February 2013; Secretary of Defense, "Actions to Improve Defense Support in Complex Catastrophes," memorandum, July 20, 2012.

[41] Graham T. Allison, *Essence of Decision: Explaining the Cuban Missile Crisis*, New York: HarperCollins, 1971, p. 176.

[42] DoD, 2013, p. 1.

[43] OSD, "Planning to Support the Department of Homeland Security," memorandum, May 2013; DoD, *Quadrennial Defense Review 2014*, Washington, D.C., 2014, p. 33.

and the 2015 *National Military Strategy* both list the priority of DSCA as number 11 out of the 12 missions listed.[44]

In addition, part of the challenge may stem from the fact that standard DSCA and DSCA for rare but extremely high-impact "complex catastrophes" are often lumped together, when, in fact, the latter can pose a far greater threat to the nation's people and property. For example, while responding to a wildfire may be a relatively low DoD priority, responding to a 9.0 earthquake in densely populated Southern California would be a high priority indeed. Paul Stockton, former Assistant Secretary of Defense for Homeland Defense and Americas' Security Affairs, established a working group for Defense Support in Complex Catastrophes in a 2011 memo, noting "The Department of Defense is well prepared to support civil authorities in normal disasters; however, when it comes to supporting complex catastrophes, there is more work to be done."[45] Our interviews and review of congressional testimony reinforced the critical importance and challenges inherent in this task.[46] In the near term, OSD should consider consolidating the various elements of DCSA guidance into an update of DoDD 3025.18 to ensure that the relative priority of DSCA is clear. In the longer term, however, OSD should consider advocating for a higher priority specifically for complex catastrophic DSCA in future high-level national security guidance.

Sourcing of DoD Forces for DSCA Missions[47]

Several USNORTHCOM interviewees advocated for assigning more forces to support the DSCA mission. Otherwise, they argued, too much time is consumed by the Global Force Management (GFM) process. Normally, they said, USNORTHCOM submits a request for forces to the GFM. Sourcing then takes several days. The interviewees asserted that, when time required for movement is factored in, for no-notice catastrophes, it will typically be three to five days before federal military forces arrive at the disaster location.[48] USNORTHCOM interviewees also suggested that a system of "geographically proximate sourcing" should be developed to speed up employment time. Typically, GFM is sourcing outside-the-continental-United-States missions in Afghanistan and elsewhere overseas, where the location of the forces being deployed is irrelevant to the response. For DSCA, location makes a big difference in response time.[49]

OSD and Joint Staff interviewees disagreed with these assertions, but from different perspectives. Some Joint Staff personnel said that the normal GFM process would be speeded up in case of a catastrophe but that FEMA should be informed not to expect federal military

---

[44] DoD, 2014, pp. 60–61; Joint Chiefs of Staff, 2015, p. 11.

[45] Paul N. Stockton, "Working Groups for Defense Support in Complex Catastrophes," memorandum, U.S. Department of Defense, October 11, 2011. Cited in Paul McHale, "Critical Mismatch: The Dangerous Gap Between Rhetoric and Readiness in DOD's Civil Support Missions," Heritage Foundation, August 13, 2012.

[46] OSD interviews, May 19, 2015; Robert G. Salesses and Joseph E. Whitlock, testimony before the Committee on Homeland Security, Subcommittee on Emergency Preparedness, Response, and Communications, U.S. House of Representatives, June 10, 2015.

[47] The sourcing of DoD forces for DSCA in the USNORTHCOM AOR was the topic with the most variation in opinions among the stakeholders we interviewed. As noted previously, we report but do not attempt to adjudicate the disparities we identified.

[48] Sourcing does not appear to be an issue for USPACOM because it has significant forces assigned to it because of its war-fighting missions.

[49] USNORTHCOM interviews, December 16, 2014.

forces in less than 72 to 96 hours in the case of a no-notice event.[50] OSD staff stated that, in the event of a no-notice catastrophe, sourcing could be accelerated through the use of a Secretary of Defense special orders book and that geographic proximity is already accepted as a selection criterion for DSCA sourcing. Additionally, they noted that the USNORTHCOM commander is authorized to employ CBRN forces for DSCA.[51]

The DSCA standing EXORD authorizes USNORTHCOM and USPACOM to place assigned forces on prepare-to-deploy order (PTDO) status and to deploy and employ them, and to place allocated forces on PTDO status. Those assigned and allocated forces are known as Category 1 forces. Additionally, there are Category 2 "Pre-Identified Resources."[52] The supported CCDR is authorized to coordinate directly with the force providers for their sourcing and place these units on a 24-hour PTDO status for up to seven days. Joint Staff planners believe this provides sufficient resources to USNORTHCOM; yet, USNORTHCOM planners we spoke with indicated they did not believe the current level of resources and their timeliness would be sufficient in case of a complex catastrophe. In particular, USNORTHCOM interviewees posited that the lack of ability to exercise and coordinate planning in advance with higher-level headquarters—i.e., those commanded by a two-star or three-star general officer/flag officer—would impede the timeliness of response and the efficiency of execution after forces are sourced.[53]

Further discussion with Joint Staff personnel indicated that the sourcing process currently uses software called Preferred Force Generation (PFG), which is a program of record that includes geographic location as a criterion and is frequently used by USPACOM.[54] Additionally, the Joint Staff is developing a new initiative called Joint Capability Support to National Emergencies (JCStoNE). JCStoNE is a PFG enhancement that provides the DSCA planner an automated process to identify (military and civilian) capabilities and allow informed preferred force/asset selection. It is designed to improve timeliness and effectiveness of DoD crisis support in complex catastrophe scenarios by allowing planners to be able to visualize the incident location and rapidly identify the full range of capable, available, and ready assets most appropriate for incident response. It will be able to ingest structured DoD data from such systems as the Joint Operation Planning and Execution System (JOPES), the Joint Capabilities Requirements Manager (JCRM), and PFG, as well as unstructured data (weather, seismic, hospital, infrastructure status, etc.) from other government agencies and civilian sites to support crisis situation awareness and response. It allows for the development of force lists and rapid export of those lists to JOPES, JCRM, and/or the Joint Flow and Analysis System for Transportation.[55]

---

[50] Joint Staff interviews, October 24, 2014. A DoD commenter noted that, under GFM business rules, sourcing could be accomplished within 24 hours, with units arriving up to 72 hours later, depending upon physical movement requirements.

[51] OSD interviews, November 24, 2014, February 5, 2015, and May 19, 2015; G3/WHEM interviews, April 16, 2015.

[52] Joint Staff interviews, June 5, 2015. There are also Category 3 forces, only for DoD internal use, and Category 4 forces, for large-scale response that require Secretary of Defense approval to place on a PTDO, deploy, or employ.

[53] USNORTHCOM interviews, December 16, 2014; Joint Staff interviews, June 5 and June 9, 2015. Also as noted in Chapter Three, FEMA officials have also expressed uncertainty regarding senior (i.e. two- and three-star level) command-and-control arrangements (FEMA interviews, April 24, 2015).

[54] The PFG was fielded in early 2015, a few months after we had conducted our USNORTHCOM interviews. (Joint Staff interview, June 9, 2015.)

[55] Joint Staff email, June 16, 2015.

Our research was unable to resolve this disparity in perceptions, but we believe both points of view proceed from untested assumptions. The most recent disaster that entailed significant use of federal military forces was Hurricane Sandy in October 2012. We assess that this event was not a reliable test of the GFM process for DSCA sourcing, because the track of the hurricane provided several days of notice before landfall. However, several CCMD and DCE interviewees stated they were not aware that the GFM process is routinely exercised during Ardent Sentry and Vigilant Shield. Instead, they believed that the sourcing of forces for exercises was assumed within the exercise scenario, so that the process did not get tested, and DoD response times were therefore not realistic.[56]

Thus, the challenge is determining whether current force assignments and sourcing processes for DSCA would be sufficient to meet the demand for DoD forces following a complex catastrophe. Tabletop or other exercises employing a complex catastrophe scenario could be used to specifically test whether present systems would be sufficient.

Conflicting Objectives of DSCA Exercises Between DoD and FEMA

Virtually all military interviewees stated that interagency exercises were productive and regularly used to test DSCA plans. CCMD staffs frequently use after action reviews to identify the need for adjustments to DSCA plans. However, some FEMA officials reported that they perceived a divergence between DoD and FEMA objectives for emergency response exercises. They stated that FEMA often struggles to conduct exercises with DoD. While FEMA would like to validate every plan with an accompanying exercise, officials asserted that this cannot always be accomplished. They perceived that DoD has a tendency to add additional circumstances to the scenario, rather than running through the exercise as originally designed by FEMA. FEMA officials said they recognize that DoD has its own methodology in place, but argued that this is all the more reason why it is important to include this consideration in exercise design: DoD infrastructure might not dovetail into FEMA plans.[57]

These observations raise the question: Is the primary purpose to validate existing plans or to test them by creating a scenario that adds unexpected challenges?[58]

Interviews with DCOs and DCE personnel appeared to reflect the perception of divergent views between FEMA and military personnel.[59] They reported that FEMA and military personnel have different cultures in regards to planning and that this is naturally reflected in how plans are exercised. Some DCE personnel perceived that FEMA planning is focused on generating mission assignments and "maintaining the checkbook" to provide reimbursement rather than anticipating the identification and movement of resources in advance. One interviewee described the problem as "FEMA catastrophic response plans are checklists, not plans."

---

[56] OSD interviews, November 24, 2014, February 5, 2015, and May 19, 2015; USNORTHCOM interviews, December 16, 2014; G3/WHEM interview, April 16, 2015. The Joint Staff interviewee on June 5, 2015, reported that, contrary to some perceptions, DSCA sourcing was indeed included during national-level exercises, such as Ardent Sentry and Vigilant Shield: "the CCMD asks for a force and a decision is made. If the decision is "no," that doesn't mean the sourcing process wasn't exercised." However, subsequent DoD commenters stated with confidence that the GFM process was not exercised during Ardent Sentry 15. We were unable to determine the facts of the case but suggest that the divergence of perceptions illustrates the challenge.

[57] Interview with FEMA officials, April 24, 2015.

[58] It could also be argued that a primary purpose of the exercises is to build relationships and familiarity between the various participants at both the institutional and individual levels.

[59] DCE interviews, June 3, 2015.

According to this perspective, military planning focuses on the movement (or maneuver) of resources and developing contingencies for surprising situations. Military personnel tend to be interested in scenarios that include unexpected events and testing contingency plans, while FEMA personnel wish to focus on executing a planned scenario and rehearsing established processes. While recognizing these differences in approach, military interviewees at multiple levels stated they had not experienced any significant problems in meeting both FEMA and military organizational objectives during exercises.[60] Nevertheless, the perception by some FEMA planners that DoD is unresponsive to their views on exercise objectives could hamper interagency collaboration in the development of integrated plans and in practicing their execution. The CCMDs and Joint Staff should consider ways to better ensure FEMA objectives are fully incorporated into the design of DSCA exercises.

Dual-Status Commander

Nonfederalized National Guard forces provide support to state emergency management agencies under the command of their respective governors, usually in a state active duty status or, when authorized by the Secretary of Defense to perform DSCA in such a status, under Title 32 of the U.S. Code. Nonfederalized National Guard forces and federal (Title 10) military forces will typically operate in parallel chains of command, as illustrated in Figure 3.5.

Because the National Guard consists of military forces, even though they are not normally *federal* Title 10 military forces, a chain of command that reports to a state governor instead of the President of the United States presents a challenge to unity of effort. The construct of a dual-status commander (DSC) was developed as a command-and-control option to address this dilemma. Appendix C of JP 3-28 (2013, p. C-1) states that:

> A DSC is a commissioned officer of the Regular Army or Air Force or a federally recognized ARNG or ANG officer authorized, pursuant to Title 32, USC, Section 315 or 325, by [the Secretary of Defense], with the consent of the applicable governor of a state, to exercise command on behalf of, and receive separate orders from, a federal chain of command and exercise command on behalf of, and receive separate orders from, a state chain of command.
>
> A DSC is an intermediate link in two distinct, separate chains of command flowing from different federal, territorial, and state governments. Although the DSC is empowered to exercise command on behalf of, and may receive orders from, two separate chains of command, those chains of command must recognize and respect the DSC's duty to exercise all authority in a completely mutually exclusive manner, i.e., either in a federal or state capacity, giving orders on behalf of or relaying orders from the federal chain of command to federal military forces and giving orders on behalf of or relaying orders from the state chain of command to state military forces, but never relaying federal orders to state military forces or state orders to federal military forces.

Figure 3.6 illustrates the DSC command structure.

---

60 USNORTHCOM interviews, December 16, 2014; G3/WHEM interview, April 16, 2015; DCE interviews, June 3, 2015.

Figure 3.5
Example of Parallel Command Structure

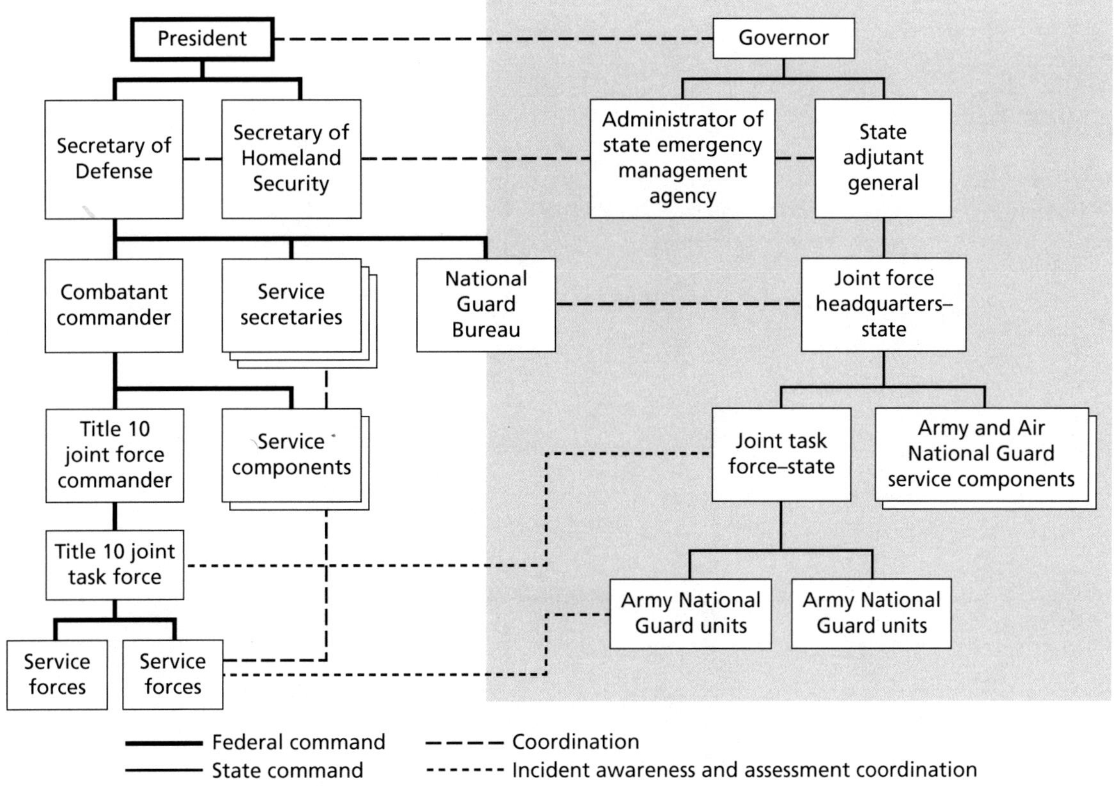

SOURCE: ADRP 3-28, 2013, p. 3-9.
NOTES: This is a simplified diagram. The Secretary of Defense typically communicates with the governor, rather than the state emergency manager or adjutant general. NGB communicates with the state adjutant general and the joint force headquarters for the state. The CCMD communicates with the state adjutant general.
RAND *RR1301-3.5*

Various interviewees said that the DSC concept is[61]

- "much ado about nothing" because it is a political issue rather than an operational issue.
- a concept that has worked thus far but has not been adequately tested in a multistate/multiregion catastrophe.
- a structure that has been proven to work very well.
- a recipe for failure.

We did not attempt to adjudicate the differences in perceptions. However, due to the variance of opinions on the topic and the potential for it to be ineffective during a multistate complex catastrophe, we assess that the issue of DSC constructs—and, more importantly, implementation of unity of effort principles more broadly—deserves further exploration.

---

[61] NGB interviews, November 5, 2014; OSD interviews, November 24, 2014, February 5, 2015, and May 19, 2015; USNORTHCOM interviews, December 16, 2014; G3/WHEM interview, April 16, 2015; a DoD commenter on the draft report.

Figure 3.6
Example Dual-Status Command Structure

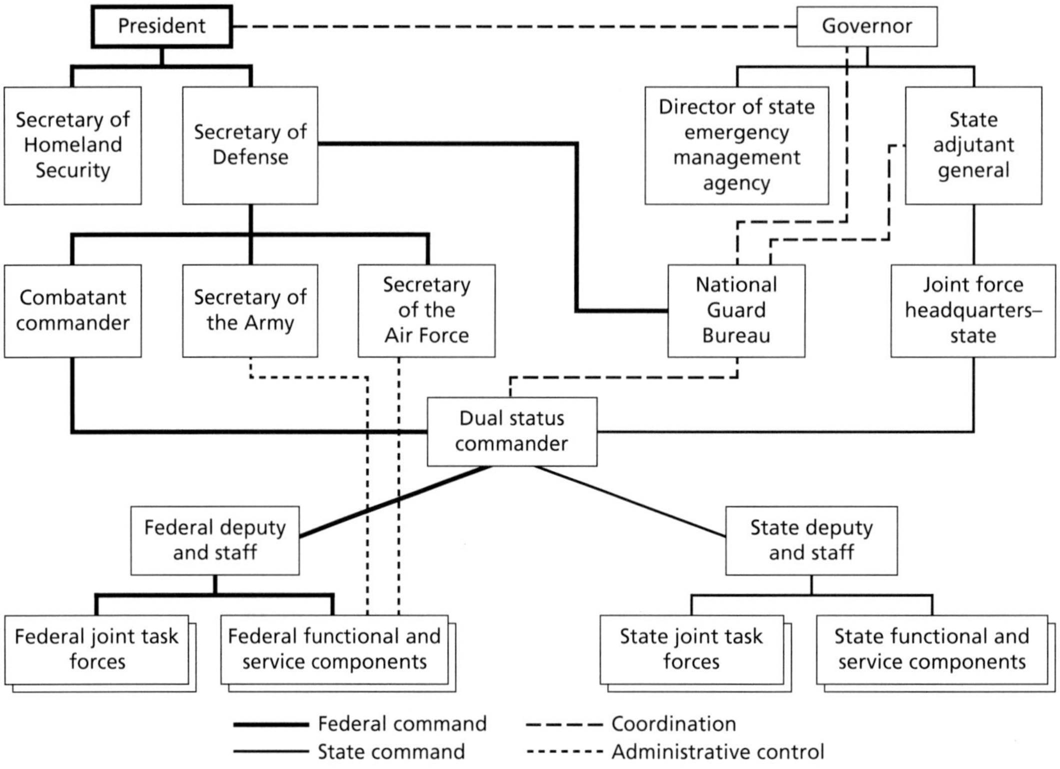

SOURCE: ADRP 3-28, 2013, p. 3-10.
NOTES: This is a simplified diagram. The Secretary of Defense typically communicates with the governor, rather than the state emergency manager or adjutant general. NGB communicates with the state adjutant general and the Joint Force headquarters for the state. The CCMD communicates with the state adjutant general.
RAND *RR1301-3.6*

Lack of Visibility of Installation- and Unit-Level Immediate Response Plans and Activities

Virtually all the key DSCA stakeholders we interviewed indicated that their organizations had no visibility on installation and unit plans for carrying out immediate response as authorized by DoDD 3025.18, which provides the following definition (p. 16):

> Immediate response authority. A Federal military commander's, DoD Component Head's, and/or responsible DoD civilian official's authority temporarily to employ resources under their control, subject to any supplemental direction provided by higher headquarters, and provide those resources to save lives, prevent human suffering, or mitigate great property damage in response to a request for assistance from a civil authority, under imminently serious conditions when time does not permit approval from a higher authority within the United States. Immediate response authority does not permit actions that would subject civilians to the use of military power that is regulatory, prescriptive, proscriptive, or compulsory.

Some of the stakeholders argued that immediate response by DoD installations could or would be a critical element of DoD's actions in the first 72 hours after a complex catastrophe. They believed that in, many or even most cases, DoD installations have mutual aid agreements (MAAs) with the local authorities in their surrounding communities. However, since installations are under service control, the geographic CCMDs are currently not provided information on these arrangements and will not become aware that immediate response has been initiated until sometime after the responding commander informs the National Joint Operations and Intelligence Center,[62] which in turn will inform the appropriate geographic CCMD.[63]

DoDI 6055.17, *DoD Installation Emergency Management (IEM) Program*, requires each installation to implement an emergency management program.[64] Because it involves actions on an installation rather than the provision of support outside the installation, the IEM program has a different focus and is not part of immediate response authority or DSCA per se. However, it has many requirements that may overlap DSCA and immediate response authority. For example,

- identification of essential resources and partnerships, such as MAAs, memorandums of understanding (MOUs), and memorandums of agreement (MOAs)
- collaboration and coordination with federal, state, local, and tribal governments, and other military department(s)
- at least yearly exercise of support agreements such as MAA, MOU, and MOAs, where they exist.

Furthermore, the DoD components with installations under their control are required to implement an exercise and evaluation program that includes "multidiscipline, multijurisdictional incidents" and "participation of appropriate leaders and decision-makers representing each of the emergency response functions on the installation and whenever possible, appropriate State, local, and tribal governments."[65] Additionally, the instruction requires that

> All IEM programs coordinate, where appropriate, with State, local, and tribal governments, other Military Department(s), or host-nation emergency response agencies and departments to identify and update responsible points of contact, emergency protocols, and expectations in the event of an emergency.[66]

However, other than the U.S. Army Reserve Command DSCA OPORD—which directs unit commanders performing immediate response to inform the appropriate DCO and the U.S. Army Reserve chain of command—we were unable to identify an existing mechanism or process for transmitting IEM plans to the DSCA CCMDs. This may present a challenge,

---

[62] According JP 2-01, *Joint and National Intelligence Support to Military Operations*, Washington, D.C.: Joint Chiefs of Staff, January 5, 2012:

> The National Joint Operations and Intelligence Center (NJOIC) is an integrated Joint Staff J-2/J-3 (operations directorate of a joint staff)/J-5 (plans directorate of a joint staff) element that monitors the global situation on a continual basis and provides the Chairman of the Joint Chiefs of Staff (CJCS), and [the Secretary of Defense] a DOD planning and crisis response capability." (p. xiv)

[63] USNORTHCOM interviews, December 16, 2014; G3/WHEM interview, April 16, 2015. However, during interviews on June 3, 2015, DCE personnel stated that the U.S. Army Reserve Command OPORD for DSCA directs unit commanders performing immediate response to inform the appropriate DCO and the U.S. Army Reserve chain of command.

[64] DoDI 6055.17, *DoD Installation Emergency Management (IEM) Program*, Washington, D.C., November 2010, pp. 18–19.

[65] DoDD 6055.17, 2010, p. 31.

[66] DoDD 6055.17, 2010, p. 32.

since the vast majority of DoD forces responding during the first 72 hours after a complex catastrophe could be operating under immediate response authority without being integrated into CCMD DSCA plans. The actions of local commanders in such cases might not be aligned with CCMD and FEMA priorities and thus be inefficient or even counterproductive. For example, a unit may be fully engaged in a local response effort when its resources are needed for a higher-priority DSCA mission elsewhere, or an installation may have agreed to provide staging area support to a local responder contrary to FEMA, FSA, or CCMD base support installation plans.

OSD should consider issuing guidance that directs commanders employing immediate response authority to report to the appropriate DCO and to their unit/installation chain of command and directs the services to share IEM plans and exercises with the appropriate CCMD. The intent of such guidance should not be to interfere with immediate response authority or IEM, but to ensure awareness of DSCA relevant plans and activities by the CCMD and DCO.

CHAPTER FOUR

Recommendations for Improving DoD Support to FEMA

Overview

Standard DSCA is an imperfect term, since DSCA by federal military forces should in general occur only when state assets are overwhelmed and FEMA requests support from DoD under the provisions of the Stafford Act following the declaration of a disaster.[1] Nonetheless, since Hurricane Katrina, DoD processes and plans have improved to such a degree that, in most cases, the DoD response can indeed be described as standard. Even the impact of Hurricane Sandy did not overwhelm DoD's ability to deliver the requested capabilities in a timely manner. However, by definition, a complex catastrophe would create a far more extensive set of demands for DoD. For example, if a tsunami on the West Coast created tens of thousands of casualties or if a nuclear device exploded in any American city, it seems likely the President would call for an immediate and massive DoD response. Thus, our approach considered DoD's support to FEMA using two broad categories: standard DSCA and complex catastrophes.

Standard DSCA

Interviews with stakeholders and our analysis of after action reports, GAO reports, and other publications indicated that standard DSCA works well.[2] While there are gaps in FEMA regional plans that could be filled by DoD, actions are being taken to identify those gaps and to plan for DoD resources to make up for civilian shortfalls. As discussed in Chapter Two, some FEMA regional plans have weaknesses or have not been completed, making the identification of gaps more challenging. DoD planners are assisting FEMA with identifying potential requests for military assistance, and planning for DSCA support, but they are not assisting FEMA with planning for civilian emergency response. There is no consensus among FEMA or DoD stakeholders on whether military planners should provide support to civilian emergency response planning. However, it might be an option for hastening the completion of those FEMA regional plans that have not been finished or are incomplete and, at a minimum, could build relationships and increase familiarity between the two entities.

[1] It can also be provided in a fully reimbursable basis during nonemergency situations under the provisions of the Economy Act (31 U.S.C. 1535). However, DSCA provided to FEMA will usually be under the Stafford Act.

[2] A detailed assessment of DoD performance during recent DSCA events was beyond the scope of this project. Our analysis relied mainly on the perceptions expressed during interviews with dozens of stakeholders at multiple echelons with DoD and at FEMA headquarters complemented by research of GAO publications and other relevant documents.

Complex Catastrophes

Progress is also being made on planning for complex catastrophes, but this is the area that presents both the most uncertainty and the greatest potential risks. Complex catastrophes represent a class of events that, in most cases, will require an obvious and immediate DoD response. The fact that they are improbable ought not to detract from the destruction that would result from such events and the urgent demands they would place on DoD. Should a complex catastrophe, such as a major earthquake along the New Madrid Fault or a tsunami on the West Coast, occur, the President and the public will expect a rapid, forward-leaning DoD response. Our analysis suggests that DoD should consider designating planning for complex catastrophes as its main effort for DSCA and clearly communicate this designation to the DSCA community.

Summary of Recommendations for Improving DoD Support to FEMA

Sustain DoD Integration with FEMA Planning

Stakeholders at multiple echelons within DoD and in FEMA headquarters reported that DSCA planning and response has clearly improved since Hurricane Katrina. Although there were some shortcomings in DoD's support to FEMA during and after Hurricane Sandy, lessons from after action reports are being applied. For the vast majority of DSCA events, planning, coordination, and execution work smoothly. While there is always room for improvement in any important endeavor, our assessment is that this aspect of DSCA currently works quite well. For example, a GS-15 FEMA employee is assigned to the J5 staff at USNORTHCOM, while officials from USNORTHCOM are embedded at FEMA Headquarters. DCOs support regional administrators. Regular communication occurs among all interagency partners within the chain of command during a daily disaster call for interagency coordination.[3]

Many stakeholders believed that DCEs should continue to support planning and exercises at the FEMA region and state levels, as well as be prepared to coordinate DSCA activities in the wake of a disaster. OSD should consider institutionalizing these activities in the forthcoming instruction that will address liaisons (DoDI 3025.jj). Meanwhile, OSD should consider reassessing DCE size and composition in terms of the variations in disaster frequency and risk between FEMA regions. Many stakeholders also asserted that CCMDs with DSCA responsibilities should continue to provide additional planning support at the FEMA region level to complement the support provided by DCEs.[4]

We identified two additional best practices in our analysis of FEMA's AHPs. First, AHPs would be more useful for DoD planning if scenarios referenced the need for specific capabilities in the form of approximate numbers (e.g., weight, distances, personnel) that might be requested by the FEMA regions, with the understanding that these would be rough estimates for planning purposes. Second, DoD should consider ways to work with FEMA to ensure that every relevant response unit has direct access to AHPs. FEMA's web portal represents a poten-

[3] Interview with FEMA officials, April 24, 2015.

[4] Although state National Guard capabilities were beyond the scope of this effort, we do note that FEMA officials indicated they were not sufficiently aware of National Guard plans. Given the primacy of the National Guard in state response operations, this would appear to be a major gap in FEMA's capability to develop comprehensive plans (interview with FEMA officials, April 24, 2015). This may be an issue that NGB wishes to address.

tially useful tool to share FEMA's plans in a controlled environment, but it must be publicized and made more readily available and user-friendly to the broader array of DoD users.

Sustain Logistics Support Planning

Rapidly moving large quantities of material across long distances and delivering them into austere locations is a DoD core competency. DoD is working with FEMA to improve planning and execution of logistics support, often using innovative approaches, such as building capability package databases that facilitate quick planning of transportation requirements. Our assessment, and that of many stakeholders, is that these efforts should be continued, especially regarding deconfliction of plans by multiple users for the same base support installation and federal staging area locations. Such deconfliction is necessary to prevent staging areas from being overwhelmed by too many responders trying to use the same space at the same time. These activities are primarily CCMD responsibilities, but OSD may wish to issue guidance to institutionalize these practices.

Consolidate DSCA Guidance That Has Been Issued Since DoDD 3025.18 Was Published in September 2012

DoD should consider publishing an update of DoDD 3025.18 that

- incorporates subsequent guidance from the relevant Secretary of Defense memoranda and the DoD *Strategy for Homeland Defense and Defense Support of Civil Authorities*[5]
- emphasizes planning for complex catastrophes
- emphasizes that DSCA for catastrophes remains a high DoD priority even if not one of the top ten.

Since DoDD 3025.18 is the primary DoD source document for DSCA authorities and processes, an update would be useful in clarifying relative priorities and capturing the guidance and strategies that have been promulgated since the current version was updated in September 2012. In the longer term, OSD should consider advocating for a higher priority specifically for "complex catastrophic DSCA response" in future high-level national security guidance.

Assess/Clarify/Further Expedite the Sourcing of Forces for DSCA Missions

Especially in the case of USNORTHCOM—which has relatively few forces assigned or allocated to it—quickly identifying, tasking, and moving forces to provide DSCA following a major disaster is an important concern.[6] Many of the stakeholders we interviewed were not confident that the current sourcing system would be sufficiently rapid to meet the needs of a complex catastrophe but also expressed an incorrect belief that the process for sourcing military forces to conduct DSCA has not been exercised. As discussed previously, J3 personnel said that they had indeed participated in Ardent Sentry and Vigilant Shield and applied sourcing solutions to meet the force requirements of those scenarios.

DoD should consider ways in which the participation by Joint Staff J3 GFM planners in national-level DSCA exercises might receive greater visibility among DSCA stake-

[5] DoD, 2013.

[6] As discussed previously, USPACOM has significant forces assigned to it because of its warfighting mission, and thus sourcing for DSCA was not a concern expressed by its planners.

holders. Improving awareness of the DSCA sourcing process during national-level exercises could increase CCMD and DCO confidence in the existing system and/or highlight areas for improvement, as well as test the sufficiency of the current processes.

To address concerns that the forces likely to be employed in response to a complex catastrophe will be ill-prepared for such missions, DoD should consider apportioning additional forces to USNORTHCOM plans for complex catastrophes or otherwise implement a mechanism to allow direct liaison authorization with major commands likely to be sourced in such cases. If DSCA is a high priority for DoD, then a sufficient number of major commands ought to be aware of plans for their employment in case of a complex catastrophe and periodically exercise them.

The Joint Staff should continue to develop—and possibly accelerate development of—the JCStoNE system to improve the timeliness and effectiveness of DoD DSCA following a complex catastrophe. It should also socialize this initiative with FEMA as soon as possible and explore the possibility of a JCStoNE variant to assist civilian emergency response.

Improve Interagency Coordination Regarding DSCA Exercise Objectives

In the course of our interviews, we identified differences in the planning cultures of DoD and FEMA, which lead to occasional disagreements regarding exercise approaches and objectives.[7] DoD should consider ways to encourage earlier coordination between DoD and FEMA players regarding the purpose of an exercise and documentation of the desired training outcomes for all stakeholders. Such actions may reduce some of the disharmony on this topic. This is primarily a CCMD responsibility, but OSD may wish to codify it in DSCA guidance.

Sustain but Further Test the Dual-Status Commander Concept

Our research indicated that the use of a National Guard general officer in a DSC role was successful as executed during DSCA operations, since such authority was initially provided in Title 32 of the U.S. Code, the 2004 National Defense Authorization Act (Pub. L. 108-136), and then expanded upon in the 2012 National Defense Authorization Act (Pub. L. 112-81).[8] However, a large number of stakeholders expressed concern that the response to a multistate complex catastrophe is particularly challenging for DSCs. DoD should consider testing DSC constructs—as well as the roles of Title 10 forces and other unity of effort issues—during a future DSCA exercise or conducting a tabletop or other smaller scale exercise to compare different courses of action to promote unity of effort.

Improve the Integration of Immediate Response with Combatant Command DSCA Planning

Immediate response authority is an important ability that allows local commanders to take action when the time required to otherwise carry out the normal DSCA request, approval, and tasking process would be likely to result in additional loss of life, loss of property, and suffering. We do not suggest changes that would inhibit or reduce immediate response authority. However, we assess that greater visibility of major unit and installation immediate response planning and execution could improve the speed and efficiency of the total DSCA response.

---

[7] Interview with FEMA officials, April 24, 2015; DCE interviews, June 3, 2015.

[8] See Ludwig J. Schumacher, "Dual Status Command for No-Notice Events: Integrating the Military Response to Domestic Disasters," *Homeland Security Affairs*, Vol. 7, February 2011; and Charles H. Jacoby, Jr., and Frank J. Grass, "Dual-Status, Single Purpose: A Unified Military Response to Hurricane Sandy," *Air National Guard Magazine*, March 12, 2013.

The status quo could inhibit unity of effort. OSD should consider revising DoDD 3025.18 or issuing other guidance that

- directs commanders implementing immediate response authority to inform the DCO for their regions and their service chains of command;
- directs the services and defense agencies to consolidate information from the IEM programs of domestic installations under their authority, including, in particular, any MAAs, MOUs, and/or MOAs with civilian authorities, and transmit them annually to the appropriate CCMD along with the after action reports from the exercises of support agreements, such as MAA, MOU, and MOAs that are required to be renewed yearly where they exist.

The services could also implement the above two actions under their own authority.

Specific Actions for DoD to Improve Support to FEMA

The conduct of DSCA has improved considerably since Hurricane Katrina. DoD has refined processes, implemented new procedures, and developed new strategies and response plans. After action reports from disasters and exercises are routinely used to assess performance and develop ways to improve DSCA efforts. Significant efforts are being devoted to the support of FEMA plans.

However, our analysis identified several areas where DSCA and support to FEMA could be improved. This report provided recommendations that would help DoD to achieve those improvements. Finally, although the focus of our study was on changes that DoD might make to its processes and plans, we encourage DoD officials and senior leaders with DSCA responsibilities to discuss their results with FEMA leaders and make them full partners in a collaborative process improvement effort.

We recommend consideration of the following specific actions:

For OSD/Joint Staff/services:

- PPublish an update of DoDD 3025.18 that consolidates guidance issued since September 2012, including the relative priority of DSCA within the 2015 *National Military Strategy*, and states that complex catastrophes are DoD's main effort for DSCA planning.
- Issue guidance requiring commanders implementing Immediate Response Authority to maximize communication, including by informing the appropriate DCO at the same time as their service chain of command.
- Issue guidance requiring services to consolidate information from installation emergency management programs of domestic installations under their authority and provide this information to the appropriate CCMD on an annual basis.
- Consider advocating for an increase in the relative priority of the DSCA mission as it relates to complex catastrophes to place it on par with military defense of the homeland.
- Institutionalize DSCA liaison personnel integration with FEMA planning within the forthcoming DoD instruction that will address liaisons (DoDI 3025.jj).
- Reassess DCO/DCE staffing to consider directing the services to increase the personnel authorizations for regions with greater risks, as well as making them joint organizations.

- Consider apportioning additional forces for USNORTHCOM plans for complex catastrophes, or otherwise implement a mechanism to authorize direct liaison between USNORTHCOM and major commands likely to provide forces in such cases.
- Consider accelerating development of the Joint Staff's JCStoNE system to improve DoD's ability to provide forces, and engage with FEMA in its development.
- Test the principle of unity of effort (including roles of Title 10 forces, DSCs, etc.) in a multistate complex catastrophe through smaller-scale or tabletop exercises. Incorporate legal considerations into exercise designs to evaluate the potential need for additional legal authority.
- Work with FEMA to help develop and document its approach to identifying shortfalls and requirements more accurately to ensure rapid, effective DSCA.

For USNORTHCOM/USPACOM:

- Sustain logistics support planning coordination with FEMA, particularly to deconflict federal military, National Guard, and FEMA use of resources such as base support installations/federal staging areas.
- Do more to socialize logistic support planning efforts with FEMA and other parts of the civilian response community.
- DoD and FEMA officials should coordinate on exercise design earlier to ensure both agencies' objectives are accomplished.
- Continue to provide CCMD staff planning assistance to FEMA regions—including for AHPs—to complement/augment DCO/DCE planning support.
- USNORTHCOM should complete the regional support plans under CONPLAN 3500-14 and routinize its review in the Chairman's Readiness System.

APPENDIX A

Overview of the National Response System

Examining the various elements of the national approach to preparedness provides an overview of national disaster planning and response. This appendix describes the main policies and plans that guide disaster response in the United States, and then identifies the main disaster response mechanisms used at the local, state, and federal levels. The appendix ends with an overview of FEMA authorities and responsibilities, as well as a discussion of ways in which DoD and FEMA coordinate.

National Disaster Planning and Response

Presidential Policy Directive 8 and the National Preparedness Goal

The country's approach to national preparedness was last revised in the 2011 Presidential Policy Directive 8 (PPD-8). PPD-8 directed the U.S. Department of Homeland Security (DHS) to develop "a National Preparedness Goal that identifies the core capabilities necessary for preparedness."[1] DHS subsequently defined the National Preparedness Goal as "a secure and resilient nation with the capabilities required across the whole community to prevent, protect against, mitigate, respond to, and recover from the threats and hazards that pose the greatest risk."[2] The National Preparedness Goal also identifies core capabilities across all five of those mission areas: prevention, protection, mitigation, response, and recovery (see Table A.1). Prevention includes those capabilities necessary to avoid, prevent, or stop a threatened or actual act of terrorism.[3] Protection includes capabilities to safeguard the homeland against acts of terrorism and man-made or natural disasters. Mitigation includes those capabilities necessary to reduce loss of life and property by lessening the impact of disasters. Response includes those capabilities necessary to save lives, protect property and the environment, and meet basic human needs after an incident has occurred. Recovery includes those capabilities necessary to assist communities affected by an incident in recovering effectively.

National Preparedness System

PPD-8 also directed DHS to develop a National Preparedness System to guide the necessary activities to achieve the National Preparedness Goal. The components of the National Pre-

---

1 The White House, Presidential Policy Directive 8, *National Preparedness*, March 30, 2011, p. 1.

2 DHS, *National Preparedness Goal*, Washington, D.C., September 2011a, p. 1.

3 Unlike other mission areas that are all-hazards by design, PPD-8 specifically focuses prevention-related activities on an imminent terrorist threat.

Table A.1
Core Capabilities, by Mission Area

<table>
<tr><th>Prevention</th><th>Protection</th><th>Mitigation</th><th>Response</th><th>Recovery</th></tr>
<tr><td colspan="5">Planning</td></tr>
<tr><td colspan="5">Public Information and Warning</td></tr>
<tr><td colspan="5">Operational Coordination</td></tr>
<tr>
<td>• Forensics and Attribution
• Intelligence and Information Sharing
• Interdiction and Disruption
• Screening, Search, and Detection</td>
<td>• Access Control and Identity Verification
• Cybersecurity
• Intelligence and Information Sharing
• Interdiction and Disruption
• Physical Protective Measures
• Risk Management for Protection Programs and Activities
• Screening, Search, and Detection
• Supply Chain Integrity and Security</td>
<td>• Community Resilience
• Long-Term Vulnerability Reduction
• Risk and Disaster Resilience Assessment
• Threats and Hazard Identification</td>
<td>• Critical Transportation
• Environmental Response/Health and Safety
• Fatality Management Services
• Infrastructure Systems
• Mass Care Services
• Mass Search and Rescue Operations
• On-Scene Security and Protection
• Operational Communications
• Public and Private Services and Resources
• Public Health and Medical Services
• Situational Assessment</td>
<td>• Economic Recovery
• Health and Social Services
• Housing
• Infrastructure Systems
• Natural and Cultural Resources</td>
</tr>
</table>

SOURCE: DHS, 2011a, p. 2.

NOTE: Planning, Public information and warning, and operational coordination are core capabilities common to all mission areas.

paredness System provide a consistent and reliable approach to support decisionmaking, resource allocation, and measure progress toward these outcomes (see Figure A.1).

The guidance, programs, processes, and systems that support each component of the National Preparedness System enable a collaborative, whole-community approach to national preparedness that engages individuals, families, communities, private and nonprofit sectors, faith-based organizations, and all levels of government. Ultimately, this integrated approach becomes a means of achieving the National Preparedness Goal in a consistent and measurable way.

National Planning System

As part of the National Preparedness System, DHS also created a National Planning System with the following elements: (1) a series of national planning frameworks that describe the key roles and responsibilities that are needed to ensure that the core capabilities of prevention, protection, mitigation, response, and recovery are provided, (2) a set of federal interagency operational plans (FIOPs) for each mission area that define in additional detail the roles and respon-

Figure A.1
Mission Area Components of the National Preparedness System

SOURCE: DHS, *National Preparedness System*, Washington, D.C., November 2011b, p. 1.
RAND *RR1301-A.1*

sibilities of critical tasks and identify resourcing and sourcing requirements for delivering core capabilities, (3) federal department and agency operational plans to implement the FIOPs, and (4) comprehensive planning guidance to support the planning of local, state, tribal, and nongovernmental organizations, in addition to the private sector. Collectively, the National Planning Frameworks provide comprehensive and interlocking strategic guidance on how to deliver and integrate core capabilities through each mission area's FIOP (see Figure A.2).

National Response Framework

The NRF is the most mature of the five national planning frameworks. While the FIOPs are directed to federal agencies, the NRF is intended to be used by a wide range of stakeholders, including individuals, families, communities, the private and nonprofit sectors, faith-based organizations, and local, state, tribal, territorial, insular area, and federal governments. The NRF "describes the principles, roles and responsibilities, and coordinating structures for delivering the core capabilities required to respond to an incident and further describes how response efforts integrate with those of the other mission areas." The NRF also sets the doctrine for how the country builds, sustains, and delivers the response core capabilities identified in the National Preparedness Goal.

The core principle of disaster response in the NRF is to resolve incidents at the lowest possible level and with mutual collaboration when necessary. The NRF recognizes that responsibility for responding to natural and manmade incidents begins at the local level. Accordingly, support from state governments and for additional capabilities should only be considered when local response efforts are taxed beyond capacity. If a state expects that its resources or capabilities may be exceeded, the governor can then request assistance from other states or the federal government. When federal response assistance is needed, it is implemented through the Secre-

Figure A.2
Integration of the Mission Areas to Achieve the National Preparedness Goal

SOURCE: DHS, *Response Federal Interagency Operational Plan*, Washington, D.C., July 2014, p. 2.
RAND *RR1301-A.2*

tary of Homeland Security (except for when those activities may interfere with the authority of the Attorney General or the Federal Bureau of Investigation). Figure A.3 illustrates the escalating response of incident management from the local to federal levels.

The coordination of operations occurs at all levels of government and initially begins with an incident commander assessment on the scene to assess the damage. The incident commander determines what level of response is needed to deliver the core capabilities. If response is needed beyond federal core capabilities, then a Stafford Act Response is initiated, and the President can implement two forms of federal supplemental assistance. The first is an emergency declaration, which is designed to protect property and public health and safety and to minimize the threat of a major disaster. The second is a major disaster declaration, which is implemented as a result of a disaster and helps the states and local communities respond and recover from the event. Figure A.4 shows how the level of response may escalate over time.

National Incident Management System

NIMS is one of the foundations of the National Preparedness System and provides the template for the management of incidents and operations in support of all five national planning frameworks. Originally issued by DHS on March 1, 2004, NIMS "provides a consistent nationwide template to enable Federal, State, tribal, and local governments, nongovernmental organizations (NGOs), and the private sector to work together to prevent, protect against, respond to, recover from, and mitigate the effects of incidents." The five major components that make up the NIMS approach are preparedness, communications and information management, resource management, command and management, and ongoing management and maintenance. NIMS integrates best practices into a framework for use nationwide by emergency management/response personnel in an all-hazards context.

Figure A.3
The Escalating Response of Incident Management Compared to Complexity

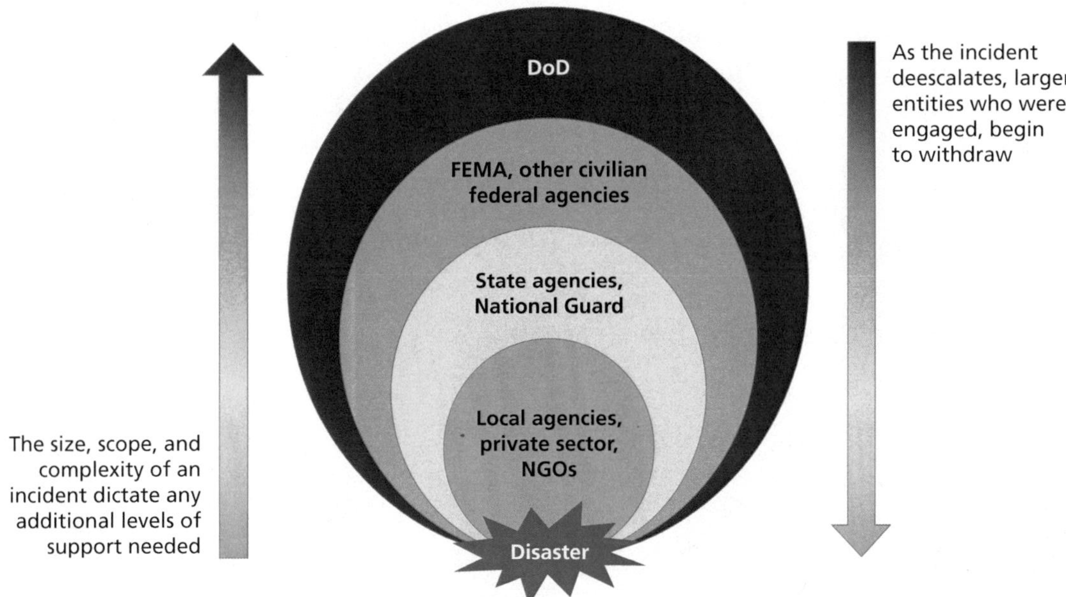

SOURCE: RAND analysis, 2015.
RAND *RR1301-A.3*

Figure A.4
The Escalating Response of Incident Management Over Time

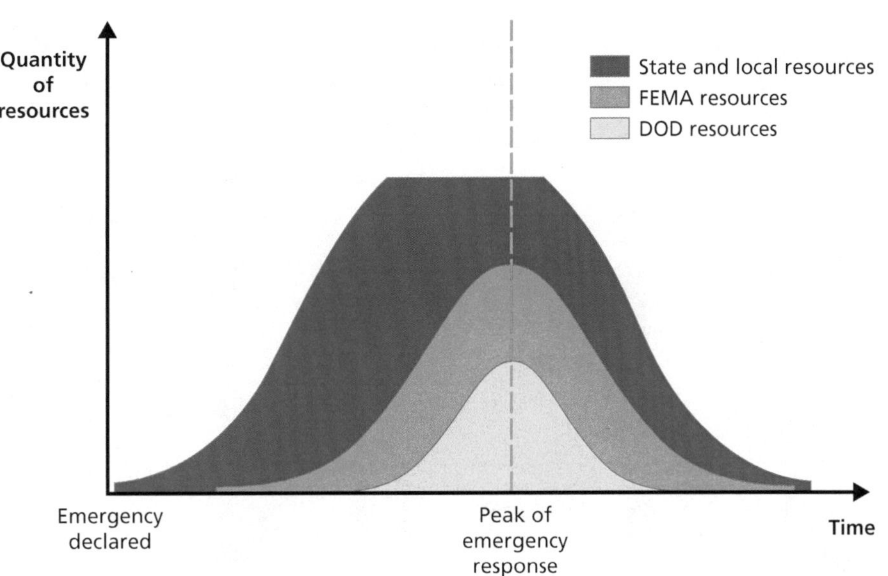

SOURCE: RAND analysis, 2015.
RAND *RR1301-A.4*

Incident Command System

Emergency responders at all levels of government use the Incident Command System (ICS) command and coordinating structures to manage response operations (see Figure A.5). ICS is a management system designed to integrate facilities, equipment, personnel, procedures, and communications within a common organizational structure. ICS is widely used by all levels of government, as well as by private-sector and nongovernmental organizations to organize field-level operations for a broad spectrum of incidents. Typically, the incident response is structured to facilitate activities in five areas: command, operations, planning, logistics, and finance/administration.

Local and State Disaster Response Mechanisms

The scale of the disaster usually dictates the level of response required. In general, local resources are always the first on scene with local public officials and their emergency personnel. Local coordinating structures are usually composed of entities that focus on functional areas, such as police, fire, public works, or emergency medical services. These are all coordinated through the local emergency operations center. Other local coordinating structures, such as local planning committees and community emergency response teams also play a critical role in local response. If additional resources are required, the town, county, or city might also rely on MAAs with neighboring localities. For some incidents, local officials can respond adequately with local resources, as well as cooperation from the private-sector and other community NGOs. However, incidents can require a statewide effort. These statewide efforts are

Figure A.5
Incident Command Structure

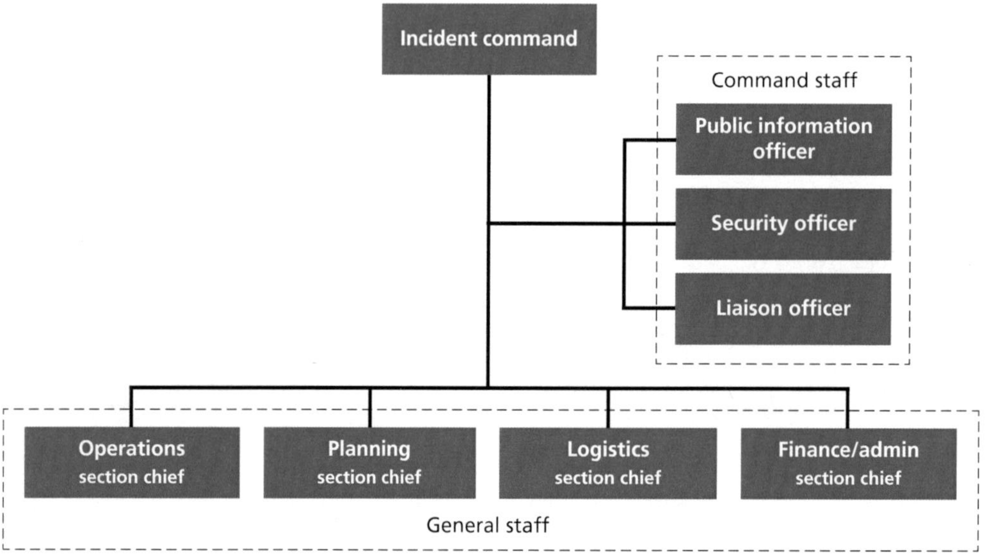

SOURCE: DHS, *National Response Framework*, 2nd edition, Washington, D.C., May 2013, p. 38.
NOTE: This is a simplified chart for one incident. In the case of complex catastrophes with longer timelines or broader geographic dispersion, there will be an "area command" above several incident commands.
RAND *RR1301-A.5*

coordinated through the state emergency operations center, which coordinates with the local response through the local emergency operations centers.

Like cities and counties, states also have interstate MAAs to request additional assistance.[4] For instance, EMAC is a national interstate MAA that allows states to share resources during a disaster. EMAC assistance can be used in conjunction with, or instead of, federal assistance. This allows the requesting state to choose the service and price from partner states.[5] Some states have also developed "mission-ready packages" that consist of specific response and recovery capabilities that are organized, developed, trained, and exercised prior to an emergency or disaster. They are based on NIMS resource typing but take the concept one step further by considering the mission, limitations that might affect the mission, required support, the footprint of the space needed to stage and complete the mission, personnel assigned to the mission, and the estimated cost.[6]

Federal Disaster Response Mechanisms

When a large-scale incident bends toward a catastrophe, federal response assistance may be required.[7] The federal response is coordinated through the Secretary of Homeland Security, whose responsibilities include administration of the response authorities of FEMA and other required DHS components. The Secretary of Homeland Security ensures that federal actions are unified and seamless to prevent gaps in federal response efforts. The federal government uses the management structures outlined in the NRF and organizes its response resources and core capabilities under the ESF construct.[8]

The ESFs organize the collaborative response effort of the federal government, and many state governments also establish their resources under this concept. The impetus behind ESFs is to bundle and manage resources around core capability requirements (see Table A.2). Each ESF has one or more agencies that are designated as ESF coordinators. These ESF coordinators oversee the preparedness activities for each ESF and coordinate the activities of primary and supporting agencies. Primary agencies have significant authorities, roles, resources, and capabilities for a particular function within the ESF. Support agencies have specific capabilities that support primary agencies in carrying out the mission of the ESF.

ESFs can be selectively activated by FEMA as needed, depending on the situation.[9] For example, during Hurricane Sandy, when one of the three major fuel distribution hubs in the country was damaged, one of the major requirements was how to facilitate the movement of

---

[4] GAO, 2010, p. 10.

[5] National Emergency Management Association, "Emergency Management Assistance Compact," 2015.

[6] National Emergency Management Association, "Emergency Management Assistance Compact: Mission-Ready Packages," 2015.

[7] The NRF defines a catastrophic incident as "any natural or manmade incident, including terrorism, that results in extraordinary levels of mass casualties, damage, or disruption severely affecting the population, infrastructure, environment, economy, national morale, or government functions" (DHS, 2013, p. 1).

[8] DHS, 2013, p. 20.

[9] DHS, 2013, p. 36.

Table A.2
Emergency Support Functions and Coordinators

Emergency Support Function	ESF Coordinator
ESF #1: Transportation	Department of Transportation
ESF #2: Communications	DHS/National Communications System
ESF #3: Public Works and Engineering	DoD/U.S. Army Corps of Engineers
ESF #4: Firefighting	Department of Agriculture/U.S. Forest Service and DHS/ FEMA/U.S. Fire Administration
ESF #5: Information and Planning	DHS/FEMA
ESF #6: Mass Care, Emergency Assistance, Temporary Housing, and Human Services	DHS/FEMA
ESF #7: Logistics	General Services Administration and DHS/FEMA
ESF #8: Public Health and Medical Services	Department of Health and Human Services
ESF #9: Search and Rescue	DHS/FEMA
EST #10: Oil and Hazardous Materials Response	Environmental Protection Agency
ESF #11: Agriculture and Natural Resources	Department of Agriculture
ESF #12: Energy	Department of Energy
ESF #13: Public Safety and Security	Department of Justice/ Bureau of Alcohol, Tobacco, Firearms, and Explosives
ESF #14: Superseded by National Disaster Recovery Framework	
ESF #15: External Affairs	DHS

SOURCE: DHS, 2013, pp. 32–35.

fuel to areas in need. Through ESF #12 (Energy), DoD and the private fuel sector collaborated to determine where the largest need was and how to distribute fuel to the community.[10]

FEMA Authorities and Responsibilities

The primary mission of FEMA is to reduce the loss of life and property and protect the country from all hazards, including natural disasters, acts of terrorism, and other manmade disasters, by leading and supporting the nation in a risk-based, comprehensive emergency management system of preparedness, protection, response, recovery, and mitigation.[11] The FEMA administrator is the principal advisor to the President, the Secretary of Homeland Security, and the Homeland Security Council regarding emergency management. Therefore, the FEMA administrator's duties include[12]

- assisting the President (through the Secretary of DHS) in carrying out the Stafford Act[13]
- operating the National Response Coordination Center

[10] Interview with FEMA officials, April 24, 2015.

[11] FEMA, *List of Authorities and References*, n.d.

[12] DHS, 2013, p. 18.

[13] The Robert T. Stafford Disaster Relief and Emergency Assistance Act (Public Law 100-707) was signed into law on November 23, 1988, and amended in April 2013 in response to Hurricane Sandy. The Stafford Act constitutes the statutory authority for most federal disaster response activities especially as they pertain to the FEMA and FEMA programs.

- the effective support of all ESFs
- preparation for, protection against, response to, and recover from all-hazards incidents.

In 2006, the Post-Katrina Emergency Management Reform Act (Pub. L. 109-295) clarified and modified the responsibilities of FEMA and the FEMA administrator. The act established new leadership positions and position requirements within FEMA, brought new missions into FEMA, restored some that had previously been removed, and enhanced the agency's authority by directing the FEMA administrator to undertake a broad range of activities before and after disasters occur.[14]

FEMA Planning Processes

To carry out the responsibilities outlined above, FEMA has refocused its planning efforts. Coordination and planning are high priorities for FEMA. The agency has developed a five-year time line for completion of all of its strategic plans. There are national plans for specific threats, as well as AHPs, which it believes will allow other agencies (including DoD) to identify capability gaps that they could fill.

In addition, in 2015 alone, FEMA had over 350 exercises planned. This exercise schedule is preparing all interagency partners to line up resources in order to avoid difficulties employing those capabilities during an actual incident.[15] Conducting exercises with DoD also assists FEMA in developing a deeper understanding of what will be needed from DoD and how to request what is needed more effectively. For example rather than requesting a particular asset (e.g., two helicopters), FEMA has instead begun to request specific capabilities (e.g., search and rescue or airlift) to better align with DoD's approach to planning.

To

> compress DoD response timelines and expedite the mission assignment request and approval process, FEMA and DoD developed 28 pre-scripted mission assignments (PSMAs) that remain working drafts based on lessons learned from previous disasters. Although not pre-approved, PSMAs facilitate a more rapid response by standardizing the process of developing Mission Assignments. They specify what type of assistance is required (personnel and equipment), identify a statement of work, and provide projected costs.[16]

Perspectives differed across our DoD and FEMA interviewees regarding the effectiveness of PSMAs. Some of our interviewees indicated that they thought that PSMAs facilitate faster processing of mission assignments, while others indicated that they have not proven to be very helpful. The concern remains that FEMA has not developed and documented its approach to identify shortfalls and develop requirements accurately enough to ensure rapid, effective DSCA.

FEMA has also recently established a "preloaded bucket" system to meet large catastrophic needs based on specific scenarios, such as earthquakes or hurricanes. These capabilities are binned into preauthorized "buckets" and sent out as one mission assignment rather than

---

[14] Keith Bea, *Federal Emergency Management Policy Changes After Hurricane Katrina: A Summary of Statutory Provisions*, Washington, D.C.: Congressional Research Service, RL33729, November 15, 2006.

[15] Interview with FEMA officials, February 26, 2015.

[16] Robert J. Fenton, "Defense Support of Civil Authorities: A Vital Resource in the Nation's Homeland Security Missions," statement before the Committee on Homeland Security Subcommittee on Emergency Preparedness, Response, and Communications, U.S. House of Representatives, Washington, D.C., June 10, 2015.

multiple mission assignments that each need authorization.[17] While this mechanism has not yet been tested in an actual incident, the hope is that this will speed up the process and allow FEMA to move needed resources to the incident scene with greater speed.[18]

Coordination Between FEMA and DoD

Recent presidential administrations have taken direct measures to foster better coordination between FEMA and DoD, as well as the National Guard, in the wake of complex catastrophes such as 9/11 and Hurricane Katrina. PPD-8 has strengthened links between DoD, federal agencies, and FEMA regional offices to foster better cooperation in response to disasters.[19] In particular, DCEs have been placed with FEMA regional offices to foster collaboration and communication with DoD, while joint force headquarters fill this role for the National Guard in each state. In addition, a DCO from ARNORTH is permanently assigned to each of the ten FEMA regions and serves as the single point of contact at the joint field offices that are established in a disaster response scenario.[20] The DCOs represent a critical link between FEMA and DoD, and the strength of this connection will influence the effectiveness of communication and coordination between the two organizations when called on to act jointly in response to a catastrophic event.

In addition to the DCOs, DoD EPLOs are authorized for each of the respective military branches in each FEMA region. While the DoD EPLOs are under the tactical control of DCOs in emergencies, the fact that they still report to their respective services otherwise remains a potential conflict in terms of chain of command and clear lines of authority. Regional EPLOs are reservists who are also embedded with the ten ARNORTH DCEs and operate under the direction of the DCO.

In addition to the DCE, a homeland response force (established in fiscal years 2011 and 2012) has been placed in one state in each of the ten FEMA regions to respond to CBRN-related contingencies.[21] Homeland response forces are National Guard–sourced and each consist of 570 individuals. They have an estimated response time of six to 12 hours and are intended to provide the initial military response after a CBRN incident.[22] The homeland response forces are intended to provide an additional coordination mechanism between DoD and FEMA to provide faster military response capabilities after a CBRN event.

---

[17] Mission assignments are work orders issued by FEMA to other federal agencies that direct the completion of a specific task and are intended to meet urgent, immediate, and short-term needs.

[18] Interview with FEMA officials, February 26, 2015.

[19] The White House, 2011.

[20] USPACOM has two additional DCOs because of the distance from the U.S. mainland and the distance between Hawaii and Guam.

[21] DoD, "Department of Defense Homeland Response Force (HRF) Fact Sheet," no date.

[22] "National Guard Homeland Response Force," *Stand-To!* March 17, 2011.

APPENDIX B

Overview of Policy and Other Guidance

Overview of Policy and Other Guidance

DoD policy, doctrine, and other forms of guidance to combatant commanders and units conducting DSCA are contained in numerous documents. The following is a very brief overview of the six DoD documents we found to be the most relevant to the purpose of this research.[1]

Secretary of Defense, "Actions to Improve Defense Support in Complex Catastrophes," Memorandum, July 2012

In this memorandum, the Secretary of Defense states that "DoD must be prepared to help civilian authorities save and protect lives during a complex catastrophe."[2] Accordingly, he directed DoD to accomplish 28 tasks organized under the following headings:

- Define Complex Catastrophe
  - Expedite Access to Army, Navy, Marine Corps, and Air Force Reserves
- Better Leverage Immediate Response Authority
- Enable Effective Access to and Use of All Defense Capabilities
- Update DoD Planning Documents to Include Preparedness for Complex Catastrophes
- Integrate and Synchronize DoD Planning with Federal, Regional, and State Partners
- Enable Fastest Identification of DoD Capabilities for Civil Support in Complex Catastrophes
- Strengthen Shared Situational Awareness
- Strengthen DoD Preparedness through Improvements to Doctrine, Exercises, Training, and Education.

DoDD 3025.18, *Defense Support of Civil Authorities (DSCA)*, Washington, D.C., September 21, 2012

This document establishes DoD policy for DSCA and assigns responsibilities for oversight and execution of DSCA activities within the United States and its territories. It describes the process for requesting DSCA and the DoD criteria for evaluating DSCA requests, defines Imme-

---

[1] These also reflect the national-level guidance in The White House, 2011.

[2] The DoD definition of *complex catastrophe* is

> Any natural or man-made incident, including cyberspace attack, power grid failure, and terrorism, which results in cascading failures of multiple, interdependent, critical, life-sustaining infrastructure sectors and causes extraordinary levels of mass casualties, damage, or disruption severely affecting the population, environment, economy, public health, national morale, response efforts, and/or government functions. (Deputy Secretary of Defense, 2013)

diate Response Authority, and assigns responsibilities to certain DoD and service officials, combatant commanders, and the Chief of the NGB.

DoD, *Strategy for Homeland Defense and Defense Support of Civil Authorities*, Washington, D.C., February 2013.

The foreword states that this strategy "postures DoD to address the range of current and emerging threats to the homeland and natural and manmade hazards in the United States for the period 2012–2020, and it is in keeping with current fiscal realities." The following are highlights we found particularly relevant to this research:[3]

- DSCA is "one of the Department's primary missions."
- One of DoD's "priority missions" for activities in the homeland is: "Provide assistance to domestic civil authorities in the event of natural or manmade disasters, potentially in response to a very significant or catastrophic event."
- DoD will enable DSCA missions via these objectives: "Maintain preparedness for domestic Chemical, Biological, Radiological, Nuclear (CBRN) incidents" and "Develop plans and procedures to ensure Defense Support of Civil Authorities during complex catastrophes."
- "Promote Federal-State unity of effort" and "Conduct integrated planning with Federal and State authorities" are among the priority lines of effort.

JP 3-28, *Defense Support of Civil Authorities*, Washington, D.C.: Joint Chiefs of Staff, July 2013

This document provides the joint doctrine for DSCA. As summarized in the commander's overview, it[4]

- describes DSCA in support of homeland security and homeland defense.
- explains how DoD supports a comprehensive all hazards response to a catastrophic incident.
- discusses permissible types of military support to law enforcement agencies and law enforcement considerations.
- provides an overview of national special security events and other domestic support activities and special events.
- outlines support and sustainment considerations for DSCA.
- provides an overview of the NIMS.

It also contains an appendix on the processes for designating and employing DSCs.

---

[3] DoD, 2013, pp. 1–2.

[4] JP 3-28, 2013, p. vii. The direction to establish the framework described above was carried out through the Joint Staff issuing a PLANORD to USNORTHCOM and USPACOM, resulting in the development of new CONPLANs, 3500-14 and 5001.

OSD, "Planning to Support the Department of Homeland Security," Memorandum, May 2013

This memorandum primarily deals with DoD's response to a request from DHS for assistance with planning for distribution of medical countermeasures from the Strategic National Stockpile. However, the secretary significantly expands on the original task and directs that:

> The Department is going to take advantage of this planning opportunity by not only conducting the planning for provision of [medical countermeasures], but also planning to close a gap in DoD's regional response plans. To close this gap, DoD will establish a framework[5] for all-hazards, Total Force, regional planning to integrate and coordinate, as appropriate, State National Guard and be integrated with, the Federal Emergency Management Agency's (FEMA) multi-year regional all-hazards and region scenario-specific planning efforts.

DoD, *Quadrennial Defense Review 2014*, Washington, D.C., 2014

The QDR examined the entire DoD enterprise with the aim of "preparing the Department of Defense for the future and prioritizing our efforts in an era of fiscal austerity."[6] It emphasizes three pillars—Protect the Homeland, Build Security Globally, and Project Power and Win Decisively. Although the pillars are interrelated and mutually supporting, the first is the most pertinent to DSCA. For "Protect the Homeland," the QDR notes that "deterring and defeating attacks on the United States is the Department's first priority." The level of priority of DSCA is less clear, however, the QDR states that "Protection of the homeland will also include sustaining capabilities to assist U.S. civil authorities"[7]

As a subset of "Protect the Homeland," the QDR includes the following:

> *Support to Civil Authorities.* The Department will continue to reshape the ability of the U.S. military forces to provide support to civil authorities when needed, and work closely with the Department's domestic agency partners. Beginning in 2010, the Department restructured domestic chemical, biological, radiological, and nuclear (CBRN) response forces, rebalancing Federal, regional, and state distributed military force contributions to the "whole-of-community" approach to national preparedness. In the coming years, we will build on improvements in preparedness for responding to major homeland natural disasters and man-made threats by better coordinating our pre- and post-incident planning and response activities with domestic partners.[8]

The QDR concludes with an assessment of the QDR by the Chairman of the Joint Chiefs of Staff. As part of this section, the chairman listed 12 missions in order of priority for distributing forces among combatant commanders. "Provide support to civil authorities" is ranked

---

[5] The direction to establish the framework described above was carried out through the Joint Staff issuing a PLANORD to USNORTHCOM and USPACOM and resulted in the development of new contingency plans CONPLANs, 3500-14 and 5001.

[6] DoD, 2014, p. 1.

[7] DoD, 2014, p. 33.

[8] DoD, 2014, pp. 33–34.

second to last within this list, ahead of only "Conduct humanitarian assistance and disaster response."[9]

[9] DoD, 2014, pp. 60–61.

Abbreviations

ADRP	Army Doctrine Reference Publication
AHP	all-hazards plan
AOR	area of responsibility
ARNORTH	U.S. Army North
CBRN	chemical, biological, radiological, and nuclear
CCMD	combatant command
CONPLAN	concept of operations plan
DCE	defense coordinating element
DCO	defense coordinating officer
DHS	U.S. Department of Homeland Security
DoD	U.S. Department of Defense
DoDD	Department of Defense directive
DoDI	Department of Defense instruction
DSC	dual-status commander
DSCA	Defense Support of Civil Authorities
EMAC	Emergency Management Assistance Compact
EPLO	emergency preparedness liaison officer
ESF	emergency support function
EXORD	execution order
FEMA	Federal Emergency Management Agency
FIOP	federal interagency operational plan
GAO	U.S. Government Accountability Office
GFM	Global Force Management
ICS	Incident Command System
IEM	installation emergency management
ISP	incident-specific plan
JCRM	Joint Capabilities Requirements Manager
JCStoNE	Joint Capability Support to National Emergencies
JOPES	Joint Operation Planning and Execution System

JP	Joint Publication
MAA	mutual aid agreement
MOA	memorandum of agreement
MOU	memorandum of understanding
NCO	noncommissioned officer
NGB	National Guard Bureau
NGO	nongovernmental organization
NIMS	National Incident Management System
NRF	National Response Framework
OFDA	Office of U.S. Foreign Disaster Assistance
OSD	Office of the Secretary of Defense
PFG	Preferred Force Generation
PLANORD	planning order
PSMA	pre-scripted mission assignment
PTDO	prepare-to-deploy order
QDR	Quadrennial Defense Review
USNORTHCOM	U.S. Northern Command
USPACOM	U.S. Pacific Command
WHEM	Western Hemisphere Emergency Management

Bibliography

Air Force Policy Directive 10-8, *Defense Support of Civil Authorities (DSCA)*, Washington, D.C.: Department of the Air Force, February 2012.

ADRP—*See* Army Doctrine Reference Publication.

Advisory Panel on Department of Defense Capabilities for Support of Civil Authorities After Certain Incidents, *Before Disaster Strikes: Imperatives for Enhancing Defense Support of Civil Authorities*, September 2010.

Allison, Graham T., *Essence of Decision: Explaining the Cuban Missile Crisis*, New York: HarperCollins, 1971.

Army Doctrine Publication 3-28, *Defense Support of Civil Authorities*, Washington, D.C.: Department of the Army, July 2012.

Army Doctrine Reference Publication 1-02, *Terms and Military Symbols*, Washington, D.C.: Department of the Army, February 2015.

Army Doctrine Reference Publication 3-28, *Defense Support of Civil Authorities*, Washington, D.C.: Department of the Army, June 2013.

Bay Area Urban Areas Security Initiative, *Regional Catastrophic Earthquake Logistics Response Plan*, April 2013.

Bea, Keith, *Federal Emergency Management Policy Changes After Hurricane Katrina: A Summary of Statutory Provisions*, Washington, D.C.: Congressional Research Service, RL33729, November 15, 2006.

Bowman, Steve, Lawrence Kapp, and Amy Belasco, *Hurricane Katrina: DOD Disaster Response*, Washington, D.C.: Congressional Research Service, RL33095, October 2005.

Brown, Jared T., *Deployable Federal Assets Supporting Domestic Disaster Response Operations: Summary and Considerations for Congress*, Washington, D.C.: Congressional Research Service, R43560, May 2014.

Center for Army Lessons Learned, *Disaster Response Staff Officer's Handbook*, Number 11-07, December 2010.

Chairman of the Joint Chiefs of Staff, *Defense Support of Civil Authorities Standing Execution Order Summary Brief*, Washington, D.C., June 2013.

Chairman of the Joint Chiefs of Staff Instruction 3125.01D, *Defense Response to CBRN Incidents in the Homeland*, Washington D.C., May 2015. Chief of Naval Operations Instruction 3440.16D, *Navy Defense Support of Civil Authorities Program*, Washington, D.C.: Department of the Navy, June 2009.

Dall, Nicholas K., *The Department of Defense Chemical, Biological, Nuclear and High Yield Explosive Response Enterprise: Have We Learned the Lessons to Ensure an Effective Response?* Fort Leavenworth, Kan.: Army Command and General Staff College, master's thesis, 2011.

Department of Defense Directive 3025.18, *Defense Support of Civil Authorities (DSCA)*, Washington, D.C., September 21, 2012.

Department of Defense Directive 5105.83, *National Guard Joint Force Headquarters—State*, Washington, D.C., January 2011.

Department of Defense Instruction 3003.01, *DoD Support to Civil Search and Rescue (SAR)*, Washington, D.C., September 2011.

Department of Defense Instruction 3020.47, *DoD Participation in the National Exercise Program (NEP)*, Washington, D.C., January 2009.

Department of Defense Instruction 3025.16, *Defense Emergency Preparedness Liaison Officer (EPLO) Programs*, Washington D.C. September 2011.

Department of Defense Instruction 6055.17, *DoD Installation Emergency Management (IEM) Program*, November 2010.

Department of the Army, "Department of the Army Financial Management Guidance for Disaster Relief Operations," memorandum, February 2014.

Deputy Secretary of Defense, "Definition of the Term Complex Catastrophe," memorandum for Secretaries of the Military Departments, Washington, D.C., February 19, 2013.

DHS—*See* U.S. Department of Homeland Security.

DoD— *See* U.S. Department of Defense.

DoDD—*See* Department of Defense Directive.

DoDI—*See* Department of Defense Instruction.

Elsea, Jennifer K., and R. Chuck Mason, *The Use of Federal Troops for Disaster Assistance: Legal Issues*, Washington, D.C.: Congressional Research Service, RS22266, November 2008.

Emergency Management Assistance Compact, website, no date. As of October 19, 2015: http://www.emacweb.org.

Federal Emergency Management Agency, *List of Authorities and References*, no date. As of October 15, 2015: http://www.fema.gov/pdf/emergency/nrf/nrf-authorities.pdf

———, *Region III All-Hazards Operational Plan*, December 2009.

———, *Developing and Maintaining Emergency Operations Plans*, CPG 101, November 2010.

———, *FEMA Incident Management and Support Keystone,* January 2011.

———, *IS-75: Military Resources in Emergency Management*, May 2011.

———, *Region VIII Regional All-Hazards Plan*, May 2011.

———, *Region II All-Hazards Plan*, April 2012.

———, *Region V All-Hazards Response Plan*, September 2012.

———, *Region IV All-Hazards Plan*, November 2012.

———, *Region VI All-Hazards Plan*, March 2013.

———, *Region IX All-Hazards Plan*, April 2013.

———, *Improvised Nuclear Device Response and Recovery,* June 2013.

——— *Hurricane Sandy After-Action Report*, July 2013.

———, *Region I All-Hazards Plan*, September 2013.

———, *Region X All-Hazards Plan*, January 2015.

FEMA—*See* Federal Emergency Management Agency.

Fenton, Robert J., "Defense Support of Civil Authorities: A Vital Resource in the Nation's Homeland Security Missions," statement before the Committee on Homeland Security Subcommittee on Emergency Preparedness, Response, and Communications, U.S. House of Representatives, Washington, D.C., June 10, 2015.

Ford, Frank, "US Army Corps of Engineers Disaster Response Missions, Roles & Readiness," presentation, U.S. Army Corps of Engineers, March 2010.

GAO—*See* U.S. Government Accountability Office.

Hasle, Carlton Wade, *Department of Defense Doctrine Should Incorporate Sixty Years of Disaster Research in Order to Realistically Plan and Effectively Execute Disaster Response*, Washington, D.C.: National Defense University, Joint Forces Staff College, June 2013.

Jackson, Brian A., Kay Sullivan Faith, and Henry H. Willis, *Evaluating the Reliability of Emergency Response Systems for Large-Scale Incident Operations*, Santa Monica, Calif. RAND Corporation, MG-994-FEMA, 2010. As of October 15, 2015:
http://www.rand.org/pubs/monographs/MG994.html

Jacoby, Charles H., Jr., and Frank J. Grass, "Dual-Status, Single Purpose: A Unified Military Response to Hurricane Sandy," *Air National Guard Magazine*, March 12, 2013. As of October 19, 2015:
http://www.ang.af.mil/news/story.asp?id=123339975

Joint Chiefs of Staff, *The National Military Strategy of the United States of America*, Washington, D.C., 2015.

Joint Publication 2-01, *Joint and National Intelligence Support to Military Operations*, Washington, D.C.: Joint Chiefs of Staff, January 5, 2012.

Joint Publication 3-26, *Defense Support of Civil Authorities*, Washington, D.C.: Joint Chiefs of Staff, July 31, 2013

Joint Publication 3-27, *Homeland Defense*, Washington, D.C.: Joint Chiefs of Staff, July 2013.

Joint Publication 3-28, *Civil Support*, Washington, D.C.: Joint Chiefs of Staff, September 2007.

Joint Publication 3-28, *Defense Support of Civil Authorities*, Washington, D.C.: Joint Chiefs of Staff, July 2013.

Joint Publication 5-0, *Joint Operation Planning*, Washington, D.C.: Joint Chiefs of Staff, August 11, 2011.

JP—*See* Joint Publication.

Kirschbaum, Joseph W, *Civil Support: DOD Is Taking Action to Strengthen Support of Civil Authorities*, testimony before the Subcommittee on Emergency Preparedness, Response, and Communications, Committee on Homeland Security, House of Representatives, Washington, D.C.: U.S. Government Accountability Office, GAO-15-686T, June 2015.

Lindsay, Bruce R., and Jared Conrad Nagel, *Federal Disaster Assistance After Hurricanes Katrina, Rita, Wilma, Gustav, and Ike*, Washington, D.C.: Congressional Research Service, July 2013.

McCarthy, Francis X., and Jared T. Brown, *Congressional Primer on Responding to Major Disasters and Emergencies*, Washington, D.C.: Congressional Research Service, April 2014.

Moore, Melinda, Michael A. Wermuth, Laura Werber Castaneda, Anita Chandra, Darcy Noricks, Adam C. Resnick, Carolyn Chu, and James J. Burks, *Bridging the Gap: Developing a Tool to Support Local Civilian and Military Disaster Preparedness*, Santa Monica, Calif.: RAND Corporation, TR-764-OSD, 2010. As of October 15, 2015:
http://www.rand.org/pubs/technical_reports/TR764.html

National Emergency Management Association, "Emergency Management Assistance Compact," 2015. As of October 19, 2015:
http://www.emacweb.org/

———, "Emergency Management Assistance Compact: Mission-Ready Packages," 2015. As of October 19, 2015:
http://www.emacweb.org/index.php/mutualaidresources/emac-library/mission-ready-packages

National Guard Bureau, *National Guard Domestic Law Enforcement Support and Mission Assurance Operations*, National Guard Regulation 500-5/Air National Guard Instruction 10-208, August 2010.

"National Guard Homeland Response Force," *Stand-To!* March 17, 2011. As of October 19, 2015:
http://www.army.mil/standto/archive/2011/03/17/

Navy Warfare Development Command, *Lessons Learned from Hurricane Sandy*, Vol. 1, No. 1, Spring 2013.

Office of the Secretary of Defense, "Planning to Support the Department of Homeland Security," memorandum, May 2013.

———, "Defense Support in Complex Catastrophes Senior Steering Group," memorandum, November 2014.

Public Law 93-288, Robert T. Stafford Disaster Relief and Emergency Assistance Act, November 23, 1988.

Public Law 108-136, National Defense Authorixation Act for Fiscal Year 2004, Novemner 24, 2003.

Public Law 109-295, Post-Katrina Emergency Management Reform Act, October 4, 2006.

Public Law 112-181, National Defense Authorixation Act for Fiscal Year 2012, December 31, 2011.

Salesses, Robert G., and Joseph E. Whitlock, testimony before the Committee on Homeland Security, Subcommittee on Emergency Preparedness, Response, and Communications, U.S. House of Representatives, June 10, 2015. As of October 19, 2015:
http://docs.house.gov/meetings/HM/HM12/20150610/103575/HHRG-114-HM12-Wstate-WhitlockJ-20150610.pdf

Schumacher, Ludwig J., "Dual Status Command for No-Notice Events: Integrating the Military Response to Domestic Disasters," *Homeland Security Affairs*, Vol. 7, February 2011. As of October 19, 2015:
https://www.hsaj.org/articles/55

Secretary of Defense, "Actions to Improve Defense Support in Complex Catastrophes," memorandum, July 20, 2012.

Stockton, Paul N., "Working Groups for Defense Support in Complex Catastrophes," memorandum, U.S. Department of Defense, October 11, 2011. Cited in Paul McHale, "Critical Mismatch: The Dangerous Gap Between Rhetoric and Readiness in DOD's Civil Support Missions," Heritage Foundation, August 13, 2012. As of October 19, 2015:
http://www.heritage.org/research/reports/2012/08/critical-mismatch-the-dangerous-gap-between-rhetoric-and-readiness-in-dod-civil-support-missions

Stuhltrager, James, "Send in the Guard: The National Guard Response to Natural Disasters," *NR&E*, Spring 2006.

U.S. Army North, Defense Support of Civil Authorities (DSCA) website, undated. As of August 6, 2015:
http://www.arnorth.army.mil/dsca

U.S. Army Forces Command, "Hurricane Sandy AAR Brief," November 2012.

U.S. Army Reserve Command, Operation Order 15-060, *United States Army Reserve Command (USARC), Hurricane/Typhoon/Earthquake and other Natural Disasters Response 2015*, February 2015.

U.S. Army Training and Doctrine Command Pamphlet 525-3-1, *The US Army Operating Concept*, Washington, D.C.: Department of the Army, October 2014.

U.S. Code, Title 10, Armed Forces, August 10, 1956.

U.S. Code, Title 31, Money and Finance, Subtitle II, The Budget Process, Chapter 15, Appropriation Accounting, Subchapter III, Transfers and reimbursements, Section 1535, Agency Agreements, February 1, 2010. As of October 29, 2015:
http://www.gpo.gov/fdsys/granule/USCODE-2009-title31/USCODE-2009-title31-subtitleII-chap15-subchapIII-sec1535/content-detail.html

U.S. Code, Title 32, National Guard, August 10, 1956.

U.S. Department of Defense, "Department of Defense Homeland Response Force (HRF) Fact Sheet," no date.

———, *Manual for Civil Emergencies*, Washington, D.C., DoD 3025.1-M, June 1994.

———, *DSCA Handbook: Tactical Level Commander and Staff Toolkit*, Washington D.C., GTA 90-01-020, July 2010a.

———, *DSCA Handbook: Officer Toolkit*, Washington D.C., GTA 90-01-021, July 2010b.

———, *Support to Foreign Disaster Relief*, Washington, D.C., GTA 90-01-030, July 2011.

———, *Strategy for Homeland Defense and Defense Support of Civil Authorities*, Washington, D.C., February 2013.

———, *Quadrennial Defense Review 2014*, Washington, D.C., 2014

———, "Region II Disaster Update Brief," presentation, June 2015.

U.S. Department of Defense, Chairman of the Joint Chiefs of Staff, *Defense Support of Civil Authorities Execution Order*, Washington, D.C., June 2013.

U.S. Department of Defense, Inspector General, *Approval Process, Tracking, and Financial Management of DoD Disaster Relief Efforts*, Washington, D.C., Report No. D-2008-130, September 2008.

U.S. Department of Defense, Joint Staff Operations Directorate, "Homeland Defense Division DSCA Branch," presentation, March 2014.

U.S. Department of Homeland Security, *National Response Plan*, Washington, D.C., December 2004.

———, *National Response Framework*, 1st edition, January 2008. As of October 19, 2015: http://www.fema.gov/pdf/emergency/nrf/nrf-core.pdf

———, *National Incident Management System*, Washington, D.C., December 2008.

———, *National Preparedness Goal*, Washington, D.C., September 2011a.

———, *National Preparedness System*, Washington, D.C., November 2011b.

———, *National Preparedness Report*, Washington, D.C., March 2013.

———, *National Response Framework*, 2nd edition, Washington, D.C., May 2013.

———, *Threat and Hazard Identification and Risk Assessment Guide*, CPG 201, Washington, D.C., August 2013.

———, *Overview of the Federal Interagency Operational Plans*, Washington, D.C., July 2014.

———, *Response Federal Interagency Operational Plan*, Washington, D.C., July 2014.

U.S. Department of Homeland Security, Office of the Inspector General, *FEMA's Sourcing for Disaster Response Goods & Services*, Washington, D.C., OIG-09-96, August 2009.

———, *FEMA's Progress in All-Hazards Mitigation*, Washington, D.C., OIG-10-03, October 2009.

U.S. Government Accountability Office, *Emergency Management Assistance Compact*, Washington, D.C., GAO-07-854, June 2007.

———, *DOD Can Enhance Efforts to Identify Capabilities to Support Civil Authorities During Disasters,* Washington, D.C., GAO-10-386, March 2010.

———, *DOD Needs to Address Gaps in Homeland Defense and Civil Support Guidance,* Washington, D.C., GAO-13-128, October 2012.

———, *Civil Support: Actions Are Needed to Improve DOD's Planning for a Complex Catastrophe*, Washington, D.C., GAO-13-763, September 2013.

U.S. Pacific Command, "J91—All Hazards Working Group," briefing, March 2015.

Walker, David M., *Testimony before the Senate Homeland Security and Governmental Affairs Committee: Hurricane Katrina*, GAO-06-442T, U.S. Government Accountability Office, March 2006.

The White House, Presidential Policy Directive 8, *National Preparedness*, March 2011.

Wombwell, James A., "Army Support During the Hurricane Katrina Disaster," Fort Leavenworth, Kan.: U.S. Army Combined Arms Center, Combat Studies Institute Press, 2005.